For Calliope

Stars dance; skies move us
Weaving thought like Calliope
We measure your glimpse
Sandcastling our time here
Building a bridge to share yours.

Contents

Prologue

I wanted to write something that finds everything you hold inside you, opens up your laughter and makes you cry. If my words burn when you first taste them, I hope you understand they burnt me when I wrote them. And when you smile, we've shared something real. Sometimes the poem we write becomes more than we knew first writing it.

This is a collection of my enigmatic, melancholic, and poly-paradoxical vignettes or "little stories" or mnemonic snapshots, as you will, of the emotional turbulence that I've written about during the global pandemic, sequestered from family and friends worldwide. Some of them represent songs and moments from my past, others sang to me as I wrote them.

If language is indeed a viral alkahest, one that can potentially metamorphosize how we structure thought, perhaps poetry is the vehicle that first opens the door to what we will eventually become. Like everything we bake, including friendships and lovers, tasting our words is like saying hello for the first time; it's the sound of one hand clapping, and the echoes can follow us through time. I hope that you enjoy what I've cast on these shores and that they open up a new door for you as well.

Reading Turbulent Waves

Unlike the experience of the rush of a torrid suspense novel, Turbulent Waves is not designed to be read iteratively from start to finish. Your own emotional turbulence should determine how you navigate the various seas within these shores. To do so, map your state of mind to one of the eleven elements in the Contents and allow it to guide your sojourn.

Light

Gorgeous Mind

All these words combine
saying such that you're
an angel in my dreams
on these lonely streets
only you command.

A glance takes my breath
a smile, a crush kept.

All these words scatter
like butterflies afraid
your gorgeous mind
devours them before
they tell you
you're beautiful.

Transparent Glances

Yours is the light within
mine is a space that holds
joy is our reach across
a coda to songs we play.

Time has dimmed our tide
yet your touch remains
like stars breaching my sky
gorgeous and empyreal.

Should we never be again
our glances transparent
a deepness we share
coveting our only real.

Your Light

I've known you forever
but we've never met.
You picked me up when
I awoke and you kept me
when I was dying.

A touch from your shared
smile sparked life when
everyone else turned away.

And the light around you
shines when others
bring only darkness.

Cerulean Song

Complex focused light
you are and I'm
drawn towards your
beautiful spirit
colored in this
cerulean song.

You sing to us with
such gorgeous
enchanting words
wonderous stories
alighting here like new
snow from some distant
mountain past as we're
delighted to share
smiles for yours.

Dazzling Shadows

There you are talking to the sunlight
knowing somehow she sings for you
through her liquid eyes onto yours,
your gentle smile lit with hers.

You turn,
a look for me,
a coyish reach you make.

She laughs,
her luminescent touch
all wound around you
her song of us
dazzling our shadows.

Laniakea's Realm

They met in Laniakea's realm
eons ago, lightyears distant.
Often they would gaze across
vast beckoning starscapes,
wondering at us and
our dazzling
blue-white box of rain.

Yet they demurred
preferring to venture
their universe within,
these lonely wraiths
finding instead,
our lost memory.

Sol

She fell across us
Dancing through our midnight sky
Peeking back at Dawn
Breathlessly holding our eyes
Till she kissed all tears away.

Luminous Threads

Days come and go here
As your luminosity
Touches everyone
Weaving light like magic thread
Your beautiful tapestry.

Stars & Atoms

We mirror your real
No one really sees our truth
Until we share it
Caught between stars and atoms
Our lives are reflected light.

Glittering Pebbles

We sojourn with you
A path of shared light and joy
Days of wonder kept
Like glittering pebbles found
Your smile skies another day.

Sunglint Mirage

Mesmerized by your addictive
my eyes catch up
sunglinting across space
catching your angel.

Poetic forms crowd around us
like we're still children
they shadow our words
holding onto what we dream.

You touch down next to me
laughter simmers us
as your mirage settles
watching who I've become.

Sunstorms

Fertile soil between our toes
laughter in our eyes
a play we tempt
such is my way to you.

Sunstorms bake our light
mirroring who we'll be
living on a starshore
caught in her riptide.

Earth holds our gentle
she knows who we'll become
days are for learning
your beautiful teaches me.

Sunbeams

Come play inside my mind
taste my glance
touch me
follow these words home.

Electric you sunbeam to me
laughing with my own
hysterical ash falls around us
we move like no one.

Our jazzed crazy fingers
write of times shared
life sweeter than now
playing us over in our minds.

Stunned Light

Stunned sunlight kisses you
smiling you remind
no one captured me
like your eyes all the time.

I try catching them
shadowing these words
my mind races with yours
you know I love you.

Our night takes us in hand
your songs work on me
making love desperately
like we have no tomorrow.

Awakening Dawn

Day finds thought bound
who are we apart
minds work to wrap us
yet we cannot be boxed.

Dreaming we fall into skies
roaming distant starscapes
haunted by yesterday
pleading for tomorrow.

Night finds thoughts alone
moments while we're lost
searching and grieving
will we ever awaken Dawn?

Underwater Sunlight

Challenged you to see me
like I thought you did
riding those waves alone
waiting to find me there.

Watching days in reverse
rerun in my mind now
on shores running wild
could today ever stay?

Wandering within ourselves
these words we're drowning
sunlight underwater warms
your eyes still on mine.

Sunlight in the Rain

When you light a candle
do you think of me alone
your likes finding me
like snowflakes on my lips?

Stay and slip beside
my writes sculpting time
finding you long ago
your voice in mine.

When the candle nights
I think of you alone
your kisses leaving me
like sunlight in the rain.

Moonlight

Moon upon a cloud
shall we sing as your light
steals our eyes glimpsing
visions of us through night?

You inspire our songs
holidays remember
like children singing delightful
under snowman's gaze.

So I take your view hoping
will she look to you
wondering do I look up
at you for her?

Tantalizing Light

Your piano keys my soul
as mesmerizing light
plays from your eyes
finding mine wanting.

Caught outside time
we've been here before
chasing who we'll become
as light tantalizingly fades.

Eternal quests beckon
written in everything we see
as sighs sing like wind
silhouetting our real.

Dark Eyes

Still moving through light
time's hold long forgotten
our laughter reaches
back into who we were.

Ancient gods taught us
how do we play here
making up new rules as
your fire remakes me.

Rising across vast dawns
I measure gorgeous eyes
lost within your dark
do you remember mine?

Collapsing Moments

Ebb and flow surreal
when you know it's time
our calculus debates
do we look or measure?

Uncertainty finds us
till our moments collapse
we love the game we play
erasing yesterday's mistakes.

Your laughter delightful
taking mine tonight
measuring yesterday's
looking for tomorrow's.

Sunlight

Sunlight measures us
Mirroring who we are now
Love captures today
Embracing what we've wanted
Teaching what we need to learn.

Ancient Light

First light in our universe
even our verse was bound
uncertainty free to roam
until we found us here.

Stars sing as we're born
seeking childhood's end
remembering our ancient lives
yet always loving today's.

Young souls bind our light
sharing their moments
should we stay here
make our universe free?

Gardening Your Sunlight

If I garden your beautiful
will your ladybugs stay
If I hold your gaze
would you fall into mine?

Sunlight begging to intrude
as it kisses your lips
smiles run away with me
dancing across our eyes.

If you tender love for us
will our song fly tonight
If you flower my mind
will you stay to become them?

Poetic Eyes

I read your poem today
looking into your eyes
my melancholy yours
only tears remain.

Beautiful you are inside
your words tripping over
to come play with mine
their dance dazzling us.

Read my eyes now as
I wrote to you last night
my words mirrored there
to wipe your tears away.

Hesitant Light

How long before you've gone
days night us like sunsets
each one kissed promises
even light hesitates to stay.

All we keep lies inside
visions you've shared
paths I've written upon
stories we can't let go.

Light knows where we'll go
sheltering our dreams
casual chances rapt
wonder never abandoned us.

Sunsets

We've been apart in time
songs our only anchor
looking for friendship
each one reminds us of you.

I like the way you sing
even sunsets hold you
masks we both wear
singing who we are.

Night wraps our dreams
listening to yesterday's
our canopy of memories
togethering a moment in us.

Lost Shadows

Alone I map your words
my road pockets our steps
these days moon's waning
darkness tempts me here.

You walk ahead now
such days behind us
reminding all we made
glinting across our path.

We follow deep felt words
measuring heart's lament
singing them together again
polishing our lost shadows.

Strange Sun

Who are we walking away
knowing these steps fall
silent on our true eyes
watching as you leave me?

It's not so clear to me
all these days woven
how you can forget
under this strange sun.

I'm still here under fire
my life microscoped
do I walk away too
will we ever meet again?

Light & Shadow

We cannot see your truth
in mirrored perspective
despite our conclusion
of what is true and real.

How do we find ourselves
pieces of light and darkness
our shadows find sight
bringing us all together.

You find our real here
written in these words
such a path we follow
longing for yours.

Flowers in the Sun

Dawn of light awakens
children of the night
dreaming wondrous tales
we chase them today.

Pastures of chance fill our eyes
unbroken chains of joy
seizing our laughter
sharing your smile.

Tender love we grew
like flowers in the sun
dancing from oceans once
sailing vast stars one day.

Mirrored Light

We write our lives here
like dying flowers
such short time we make
yet yours never ends.

Someone finds our taste
she devours our real
makes these words true
reminds me of yours.

You' ve found yourself
like mirrored light we become
such imagined visions
rewriting us with your look.

Dust Upon My Mind

Seamlessly we move from thought
into your light
our words keys you find
opening perception's door.

It's a silent transformation
written across our eyes
as I move from pages
strewn like dust upon my mind.

We find purpose each day
written behind our eyes
such is this light we find
when we read yours.

Tides of Light

She knows my only touch
impossibly reach
like tides of light
flooding her eyes without mine.

Singing almost oceans apart
our songs play hard
will they stop our hearts
still trying to show us?

Baby you know me now
our voices frozen
like sand looking for a shore
drifting on a wave.

Kissing Language

I'm writing about you
your beautiful takes me
I still touch your light
keeping mine umbrellaed.

Do we play our games
wanting these crazy words
making us up each night
till we touch tomorrow?

Your language kisses me
singing us as we play
you've known me before
writing about mine.

Between Darkness & Light

Shadows bind to our light
embracing sunborn minds
alive we bridge both
between atoms and galaxies.

Where does light stop
or darkness seep inside
skin-deep or soul-deep
one holds us, one binds.

We're painted here alive
between water and air
as reason drowns ignorance
shadowing our light.

Painting Us Real

No words can ever tell
your story envelopes me
taped to my mind's wall
I read you every night.

Will you bring me home
shelter me in your sky
keep my darkness and light
take me inside again?

We paint ourselves real
like sunflowers drinking light
such lives we share
making us up each day.

Sunglassing Uncertainty

Colors your eyes paint
love a canvas we play upon
every word you make
holds my brush.

We're lost children playing
together through darkness
our light sings us
whispering about yesterday's.

Silent moves we take today
finding our minds sharing
such designs of tomorrow
sunglassing uncertainty.

Flowering into the Night

Red flowers alone await
dawn comforts them
drinking sunlight streams
till your touch awakens.

Dazzling surreal light
bakes us like no other
I feel your gaze
visions of what might become.

Deftly moving in our dance
we take hold of today
a passion play we write
flowering into the night.

Light from Other Stars

Night sky layers our thoughts
losing meaning in my words
they fall apart here
your chill ripping into me.

I don't know where we are
light from other stars
gently raining on my mind
new words search for us.

You play my song again
trying on our dance
we settle in your fire
wanting to share our light.

Othiym Lunarsa

Your river of light
carries our lost sighs
and as the sun sets
we disappear into its sky.

Kissed by Othiym Lunarsa
wicked laughter grows
shadowing us like desire
we learn our way here.

Rapt fire plays against us
like dancing on light
rippling across night's ocean
as the sun carries us home.

Sunlit Memories

Sunlight opens my memories
forty-eight hour labor
cherishes us like no one
eyes that traveled in time.

Dancing a samba all our lives
we stepped forward with her
a loving embrace around us
every song was ours.

Living in syncopated rhythm
she umbrellaed our lives
storms feared her wrath
I love you, Mom.

Chasing Sunlight

Gorgeous sunlight dances
inside your eyes
charming mine
like lightning in the night.

If you want my touch
when your sky falls
this is where I live
waiting for you to find me.

I used to write you letters
they'd fly our world
chasing sunlight and lightning
looking for your beautiful.

Silent Gazes

Silent gazes sigh
Even the day finds a smile
Knowing dear friends stay
Even under distant skies
We all sail under our sun.

Lightwaves

Waves lap across our light
caressing who we are
when you took my look
leaving me within yours.

So we spend time's now
dreaming of a shore
when stars left their mark
like sand in our pockets.

Night ripples onto us
she sings our song
when I'd hold your look
leaving you wanting mine.

Mesmerizing Light

Dawn rises touching me
thoughts wake my soul
sunlight kisses eyes
alone with today's beautiful.

Afternoon remembers you
dreams we've shared
winter's silent snowflakes
mesmerizing like you.

Evening shares her secrets
holding yours and mine
we kiss today farewell
nightfalling together.

Cool Sun Vibe

Slow vibe finds me here
wanting your smile
even as the day ebbs
you always find mine.

When my words run out
touching who we were
I know you're still there
reading who I've become.

Cool sun rains around us
as the moonlight hides
eyes dripping with envy
waiting till you want mine.

Drinking Liquid Sun

Flowers open in sunlight
kissing our delight
dark nights bloom into day
dancing around us again.

Alone within we too flower
reaching for our skies
embraced by liquid sun
mirroring who we are.

Sacred chants haunt us
replaying lost memories
days when we forgot
yours holding on to mine.

Highway Signs

Moonlight eclipsing who we are
our deserted memories
strewn across these roads
like fading highway signs.

Still you touch my deeper time
in step with what we had
days when a thrill meant it's real
rippling chills through us.

Morning's dawn kisses today
our bare feet warming us
I remember your first look
saving who I would become.

Blanket of Nightfall

You make me like I'm yours
a comfortable beach
sand finds what we've lost
waves wash what we've found.

Sipping your delightful
Luna's envy kisses us
beaming like first lovers
even our laughter bakes.

Startled stars race away
as we pull the sky over us
under her blanket of nightfall
I make you like you're mine.

A Deeper Look

Like a song we both became
I'm writing of us
as evening dusks now
lyrics bind our eyes.

Words feel who you are
they wrap inside you
making up what you dream
touching what we want.

Your eyes read mine tonight
as today fades away
we play songs to remember
poetry making us up again.

Remembering Light

Once again our eyes wield light
swords we covet to employ
cutting through glass moments
mirroring our only real.

I wanted to find you here
writing about who we've become
of days sipping our Fridays
tasting who we wanted to be.

We walked into such vastness
shimmering like our delicious
even as ghosts haunt our shadows
new dreams chase them away.

Turbulent Waves

Love comes to you
sharp breath sings
arms lost all around
turbulent waves take us.

Catching light as we look
maybe I'll just stay awhile
holding that sweet smile
moments caught in your spell.

Falling within these words
what happened to me
enchanted music you weave
sunsetting us tonight.

Sunlight tasting like you
tempts memories
beams play my eyes
rapt up inside yours.

Siren's call commands
anchoring ancient thought
left under brilliant rays
I wonder who you are.

Starlight hugs me close
whispers you once kissed
surfing my turbulent waves
you take all that remains.

Light Tides

Where have we been
held between vast realms
light tides our shores
flowering who we'll become.

Following uncertainty's guide
we sun dance
asking if we exist
measuring each moment.

Odyssey's road takes us
as starlit candles beckon
we garden our souls
across a sea of memories.

Komorebi

Crushed Sunlight

Days have taken your mind
walking alongside my words
we'd write our songs
sighing as they took us back.

When you look that way
crushing sunlight at me
such moments flee
leaving us lost outside today.

Nights have forgotten mine
lying here alongside yours
a dream of your happy
still remembers me by dawn.

I love your lyrical touch
seeing me in you
when days invited us
sharing light and gravity.

We'd write all night
scripting snow-bound days
delicious tastes we'd invent
waxing our slopes home.

You loved our rappinghood
touching yours with mine
all those days we played
crushing sunlight together.

Yesterday's Tomorrow

Moving alone apart here
into seasons of light
dazzling star rain floods us
killing these blues.

I know your dark storms
we sky our laughter there
harbored apart and alone
haunting yesterday's tomorrow.

Nights gift us each other
delicious abandon touches
despite this darkness
we move again together.

Your Gravity

Amidst these staggering tides
we navigate today
tell you I'm lost
you know me so well.

I need your gravity
couldn't say if we touched
our light interstellar
searching for ourselves.

You mapped island universes
we'd play here forever
you always found me
I've always known you.

Night

She seduces dusk's play
captivating our souls
tempted by her kiss
Day embraces her.

She owns wraith's moon
starlight scatters within her
controlling our passion
we meddle in her darkness.

She lures away our control
coveting passion's play
blanketing our wicked
till dreams of her find dawn.

Strange Days

Empty pages try to say
reminiscing your sweet
we caravanserai all night
dreaming of our world.

You take me in your light
I wonder at your madrigal
singing about days
we loved consuming us.

Want you on me again
igniting words we create
till strange days efferverse
filling my page with yours.

Strange Suns

Friday evening you're gone
I remember octobering you
fires took your loves
they came home safe.

You stopped time then
capturing mine
such a long time ago
we're not us anymore.

How do we find ourselves
under these strange suns
masking yesterday's light
like we shared smiles then?

Making Us

You live in my mind
Such words I write make you real
They dance in your eyes
Wondering if you want them
As nightfall entices yours.

Tantalizing Moments

Regarding eyes you make
mine forget who I am
tantalized moments flicker
like a drive-in movie.

Stars blanket as we huddle
wanting across whispers
your breath invites
such a dance we delight.

All our days alone
saving my best for yours
I look back remembering
you always made me.

Your Shore

We fly through the night
riding words we know
winds around take us
no one knows we're here.

Never been one to follow
night's beckoning allure
restless like the ocean
searching for your shore.

Amused you stay with me
eyeing me in Moon's light
drifting together
we follow our hearts.

Dancing Thought

Even as you piano my soul
your light captures me
like komorebi's rays
kissing leaves as they land.

Stay will you as they fly
singing a love song
even Miles played along
painting your delightful.

Our music captives today
gifting who we have become
as when you smile now
thought dances around us.

Ghosting Us

We read each other's vibe
tethered behind light
like that one glance
given when we were free.

How does sanity check in
reimagining what's real
deliberately painting over us
skating between our lines.

We ghost each other now
escaping lost seasons
days have seduced weeks
can we stop time to dance?

Crazy Rain

Cold crazy rain fell
streetlights candling our eyes
as we hurried across
night's somber embrace.

Broken flowers found our path
along these moonlit roads
they followed us home
as lingering scents.

We kiss wet lips on desire
photographing our eyes
magic elixirs to help us
remember us tomorrow.

Introverted Intuition

Words look for us
wondering do we know
what we've found through
our eyes looking back?

You take me wanting more
beckoning who we were
empathic introverted intuition
shows me who you are.

We write another dance
your words making up mine
our music rewrites us
into who we were again.

Komorebi's Laughter

Anyone can join us across
you can stay here and sing
wander into our words
write your sunlight.

Sudden joy filters down
like komorebi playing through trees
each word a falling leaf
making us up as they go.

When they fly free again
looking back at us
you'll remember me
even as they fade away.

Haunting Gaze

Relentless spacetime wields
yesterday's apocalypse
our moments alone under
strange sun's haunting gaze.

Wild astonishment shadows
as we walk upon new roads
where should we go when
one hand clapping is silence.

We struggle making days
direction's mirror clouded
leaving us distracted
nowhere left to go.

Dancing Komorebi

Years beautiful make yours
maybe I'm a moment
sand between your toes
like stars enveloping us.

Wandering our familiar
your music poetics me
a little magic binds
enchanting new skies.

Like I once pictured you
crazy strung-out dawns
our komorebi dances
even your laughter glows.

Conjured Dances

Flowers float on our smiles
riding along us in thought
they tempt us to give in
remembering those promises.

Some days lost we stayed
together on blank pages
writing like we still lived
alone sharing our gifts.

Such worlds try to fade
we still hold on dreaming
our dances again conjured
we never let go of them.

Lost in Your Storm

I don't ever say goodbye
every time you leave me
couldn't you just see
all these sighs lost on you?

When you touch my eyes
do you know I'm yours
you took me before
no shore left for my waves.

Chills find my touch now
I'm lost in your storm
find me again
against these days alone.

Black & White

Who are you soul gazing
light transparent in us
no skin shines on my mind
your love is mine too.

When we dance touching
nothing tastes like us
black and white truth equal
our eyes sing together.

So kiss me my sweet
I need you here
we will prevail over today
our earth needs us both.

Photographing Tomorrow

You fired glances unbelieving
moments held our breath
such timelessness now
remembering who we were.

I take your eyes back
mirroring shared smiles
asking should we dance
your hand finds mine.

We knew this happened
before we said hello
septembering our lives
photographing tomorrow.

Meeting Us

We share our light here
along galactic pathways
dancing with our Sun
searching for ourselves.

Sojourning along the way
we meet passing through
your wondrous lessons
taught us all how to love.

We bid you farewell now
your light we'll always keep
memories of such love remain
binding us forever.

Children of the Sun

Children of the sun
we focus love within our lives
sharing our light
across the universe.

Shadows reign around us
reshaping such visions
as we hold each other
standing together.

Centered within vast realms
we reach for our apotheosis
making our daily bread
endeavoring to be free.

Fallen Leaves

Separate realities hold us
minds reach across
words puzzle us together
days you're no longer here.

Pieces of me fall away
they've forgotten my way
such light we shared
can no longer find us.

Melancholic dreams now
rake through these
fallen leaves of you
drifting back into past lives.

Accidental Lovers

We met accidentally
our eyes never settling
my words rushing you
yours tempting mine.

They seduced us both
your mystery so alluring;
drinking wine together
we found love a muse.

But the scattered days
took us apart as our
stories drifted away and
we left this theater alone.

Slaying Eyes

Find us here sharing your song
those eyes prisoners we become
slaying our dazzle
just like your hello kills.

Treasures bound within a smile
your words a poetic dance
spelling enchanted muses
we follow knowingly into their abyss.

Seared to our souls we awaken
inside your beautiful mind
our universes collide
like sunlight in those eyes.

Moving Into My Mind

Slipping into my eyes again
you command my light
writing your poetry in me
you move into my mind.

Spaces we're sequestered
singing our songs alone
do we make us real tonight
I'm dying to find you out.

Shadows conquer my words
trying to fathom your soul
tell me what you want
you're still alive in me.

Wilder Shores of Love

Creatures of the sun we fly
on wilderness thoughts
our tides finding new shores
such dreams we take home.

Alone through the nights
remaking ourselves
you can find me then
drinking your eyes in mine.

Such wild visions are we
soaring into our light
stepping into moments
our wilder shores of love.

Sunsetting Time

Sunsetting time stole us away
photographed in love
lost in tomorrow's mirage
I saw your goodbye look.

Dark circles and shadows
paint your forever smile
like trees devouring light
I'm hungry for yours.

Our songs play me
like art binds our eyes
capturing yesterday
when you someday'ed me.

Remembering Your Beautiful

Walking in this silent desert
sing with me tonight
stars made our light
do you remember mine?

Your music made me
remembering your beautiful
I lived with your pain
sailing across our crazy.

Knowing shared spaces
you've taken my look
holding my words
do you still sing for them?

Evanescent Moment

Our lives sparkle in joy
like glittering komorebi
a reach across our minds
living enchanted tales.

Gorgeous elysian eyes
surf or reticence
like mångata's wanderlust
an evanescent moment.

Gathering light we sail
in search of a raconteur
such is our road here
sondering for yours.

Sighing Rain

Her touch pianos your words
surreptitiously binding hers
her thoughts linger there
crystallizing within yours.

Sighing rain embraces us
tears filling empty pockets
as our komorebi glistens
iridescence umbrella's us.

Sunlight rewrites our glances
uncovering these words
as we reach new skies
another day begins to sing.

Betwixting Gravity

Slipping your eyes off me
glints flick betwixtingly
gravitating now
tasting our atmosphere.

Surfaces kiss moments
a searing delicious spell
one where we forget us
blanketed under stars.

Euphoria begs to dance
winking like we're friends
she holds you closer
waiting lips sigh hello.

Dreaming Surreal

Caught by canyon's surreal
when a day meant everything
perhaps I'll find my way out
daydreaming of you.

Visions of cloudless skies
when laughter would run ahead
we'd make us up again
killin' time just to be together.

So we climbed into tomorrow
leaving who we might have been
soaring on flights of fantasy
finally free to dream again.

Mirages

Simple times how I miss
we'd catch light beams
share smiles as if
we'd live forever.

You knew who I was
seeing colors in my songs
old souls outside of time
disappearing like a mirage.

I wanted to catch your eyes
how sunlight fell into you
enchanting everyone
we all loved you here.

Nonchalant Masquerade

My brush holds your eyes
touching who we've become
pacing time like a piano
lips like a sip of brandy.

Mirrors make us up as light
our nonchalant masquerade
even your shadow wants us
as I paint you into mine.

Our glasses empty as we look
dipping into your paint
past Illusions abandon us
even our light knows better.

Unbroken Chain

Nearing a sudden touch
I turn up your song
never sharing eyes
our lyrics streetlight us.

Blurred views encapsulate
burning fuels passion's gate
laughter opens it
do you want to dance?

Like a desert moment frozen
we believe fairy tales
lost visions emerald skies
our unbroken chain.

Drenched Sunlight

Drenched sunlight saunas me
yet all I feel is you
a poem I yearn to pen
as summer says goodbye.

Autumnal dust cries for you
falling in my mind
kissing me like whispers
as we pave our road.

Mountain's fire held us
when dear ones ran
yet you thought of me
as winter made us real.

Between Us and the Light

Between us and the light
night's chill slept beside us
our play of fire
dancing with our shadows.

In our dark, sounds lure us
they play Hope's wildness
her deftness stares
commanding our passion.

We draw intuition's breath
spellbound in our real
will you help me see you
move into our together light?

Isabel

Years have become you
darling eyes bind us
shared smiles no one has
you always stay in the moment.

Little gorgeous angel
so many days to hold
even now your wonderful
laughter becomes ours.

Years have made us all
cherish your love
like the desert sky
you always paint what's real.

Calliope

All These Words...

All these words combine
saying such that you're
an angel in my dreams
on these lonely streets
only you command.

A glance takes my breath
a smile, a crush kept.

All these words scatter
like butterflies afraid
your gorgeous mind
devours them before
they tell you
you're beautiful.

Your Muse

Songs to find your muse
They seek to carry your heart
Can you find yourself
Sing your words into a poem
Writing who you have become?

Song of My Poetry

If you were a song
you'd never leave my lips
if you were a poem
you'd never leave my heart.

Song of my poetry you sing me
cut from diamond beautiful
such eyes of opal you make me
dreaming of our fires.

If I were your song
I'd play for you all night
If I were your poem
I'd never leave your eyes.

Dancing Glances

Visions of you play my sky
sunrising our eyes
dawning at first light
waking our laughter.

We afternoon coyness
languishing onto smiles
I puzzle you together as
your glance dances with mine.

Dusk holds our breath
kissing sunsets in your sky
we love playing
nightfalling alone together.

Calliope's Saudade

We soared above the clouds
rapt visions fell below
startlingly Calliope took you
as a stranger flew away.

Left with only my wings
Luna delightedly lured
casting what remained
onto your fading shadow.

Alas, muses still bear my words
they play our songs
sadly, I will remember you
as Saudade owns me now.

Sandboxing Our Minds

Of ages that have found us
through paths of light and art
holding our lives dear
never letting them go.

How do we find thoughts
those days we played
sandboxing our minds
so happy to be alive?

Evening reflection beckons
infusing within our memory
our wilder shores of love
waves still take us back.

Deep Waters

Deep water souls we are
alive in a magical galaxy
sharing our love, breath
water and light.

Dreams we surface upon
they pull us under
burning our memories
like love branded in our hearts.

Deep water is our home
darkness spans this universe
across mother stars
stay and swim with me.

Deciphering You

Your poetry washes over me
such waves you surf
chilling my memory as
I decipher yours.

We set our table together
looking for us tonight
crushing our words
learning to talk together.

Night always finds poignancy
left alone we touch
kissing words goodnight
wondering if we'll stay.

Melancholy

Storms cast me upon her shore
my lover Melancholy
eternally at my side
holds my abandoned thoughts.

Verde mar eyes found hers
as empyrean glances asked
do forever hearts live
within perpetual lives?

Deep in time's ink
I sail alone now
calm in my storm asking
will time recall us yet again?

Perfection's Challenge

Perfection's challenge waits
sensing we are but children
our creativity sandboxed
across the universe.

Waking from broken dreams
we paint us in tomorrow
our emotions unveiled
like autumn's golden leaves.

Spellbound we write
as today defines us
like a brush on canvas
inspiring our words.

Dreams

You're just a dream
I could never reach
so I sing you my days
will you find mine instead?

I write these songs so
in my night you'll hear me
and when your wings fail,
I'll carry you with mine.

Yet dreams I find upon
my skies leave me hoping
that you're real and tonight
you'll dream of me.

Calliope's Smile

Cray-cray sand all over me
dancing particles
why do they stay
breathing, seeping, becoming me.

Our laughs so chillin'
sitting next to your vibe
one way or another
Calliope shares her smile.

Running out of time again
my child still sings you
sandboxing my thoughts
holding, being, loving you.

Hope

How do we stay sane
when broken and alone
only hope kept dear and
we forget there is none.

Do we flood our mind
erasing everything with
wine, music, and words
waiting for the nevercomes?

Who are we when what's left
of us picks up these words
words still hopeful
of a fool's gold quest?

We stand with you, love
taking your hands,
hugging your eyes
making you believe in us.

Hope never abandoned you
she kept your smile
waiting when you'd know
we never left your side.

You take these words
finding yourself with me
knowing my mind, yours
and hope is always here.

Sipping Sweet

Astonished we tide time
mating our moves
do you jet lag my words
tasting our memory.

Awaiting your searing look
Château d'Yqueming now
I slip beside your smile
as we both sip them sweet.

Our wine empty we look back
ages of written pages
will you still want me
hoping we're real?

Playing Delight

Seasoned minds delicious
she devours my heart
wandering through her reflection
written all over my surprise.

We caravanserai the night
surreptitiously eyeing us
such exquisite tastes
slaying for paradise.

Euphoric lips hunger
you move onto mine
playing our delight as
your blade asks for more.

Fires Upon Our Deep

We sunset our eyes
haunting evening's beach
like stealthy waves kissing it
nightfalling our desire.

Cold surf caught us
crazy cries of delight
moments we stoked for today
fires upon our deep.

Stars unmask the night
candling our rendezvous
like footprints in the sand
leading us home.

Fleeting Dreams

All these words take us
as I find your heart
I'm senseless in this
fleeting dream of ours.

My broken angel gently laughs
as she has forever smiled
guiding me through
these lonely words we share.

Oh to see and hold yours
one more time as time fades
like my brief vision of you
in all these dreams of us.

Spellbound Apparitions

We unmask with dusk
sipping our sighs
poetic eyes rewrite us
spellbound fading apparitions.

Visions of your remark's intent
holds mine at bay
as evening ignites
you slay my dragons.

Inhibitions guard darkness
coursing uncharted skies
will dawn find us
before night lets us go?

Alone in the Night

My words lighthouse
waiting for yours
I walk away from them
wondering if you were ever here

Night sky wraps us up alone
saxophoning our souls
your breath looks for mine
steeping inside our thoughts.

How do we share melancholy
alone in the night
crazy heartbeats enveloping
as we wait on our shores.

Haunting Dreams

I remember septembering you
everyone else froze time
found you staying
words we made kept us.

Perfect against our shores
their waves sing today
haunting dreams like
photographs never seen.

All those lost sighs drift
like storms in our minds
waking us in the night
stoking our yesterdays.

Gifting Your Delight

Sunstruck frost glistens
holding your eyes in mine
we memory these times
singing our yesterday.

Snowfall theater's your look
gorgeous beautiful you share
waking Christmas morning
pajama'd cozy twinkle.

Yuletides find our shores
spirits huddled by the fire
cherishing this moment
gifting your delight.

Brilliant Madness

You won before we met
bikini' ing your brilliant madness
of sweet muse delight
playing me all day.

Smoldering crazy coals
we music our electric vibe
a dance dreamt beautiful
my wings under yours.

Visionary twin flames
can I ever let you go
cast alone into darkness
knowing you want me.

Ancient Tears

Will you make me up tonight
captain my turbulent sea
hold these waves inside
find my wanton shore?

Can I apparition you here
drink your delightful
sky my light
footprint your beach?

Your songs clothesline me
drying ancient tears
we knew meeting again
we' d heartbreak our sunset.

Dancing with Uncertainty

She glances at you
wonders of your story
hers escapes as you look
desperate for first words.

When we write today
thinking we know ourselves
our music plays us
dancing with uncertainty.

Releasing her goodbye eyes
you surrender her light
masking your sigh
sunsetting another bookended day.

Calliope's Road

Peering out your eyes find me
like misty star-lit constellations
your flight angels streetlight
Calliope's road to our hearts.

Touching down you hug me
beneath our vast universe
words fill corridors in my mind
they laugh dancing with us.

Across our touching looks
longing's sea breeze sighs
a kiss we've always met
she takes us home again.

Waves Without a Shore

October skies found us
fires chased you to me
broken steps running
we never lost our song.

Waves without a shore
brilliant mind you share
my madness, my darkness
yours asked me to dance.

We knew us many times
mirroring shared smiles
your beautiful brown eyes
always saving my crazy.

Treasures

Wrapped inside searing intuition
we walk on sacred ground
transparent days meet us
as light and darkness play.

Enveloped like precious pearls
love awaits
such vast lonely spaces
your eyes and mine.

Born of the sun unique
treasured beings
in love with your light
sharing our desperate.

Losing Forever

A second turned forever
your eyes find mine
nowhere else to go
we weigh desire's allure.

Your lips taste my words
trapped like sweetness
deciphering their charm
amused with my flavors.

Losing forever seconds tick
we fall into our futures
I grapple for mine
as your eyes turn away.

Glittering Samba

Would you dance with me
take my eyes in yours
move with me today
let my mind be yours.

Our samba play enchants
born from stars we glow
even in our darkness
your dance glitters.

We unmask through time
peering out onto vast shores
wondering as the song begins
will your dance be mine?

Savored Enigmas

Dawn draws your edges
such delicious words
like yesterday's eyes
finding new lovers.

Their ravenous appetite
scour you as each one
disappears into another mind
locking them away.

You're beautiful each notes
as they harvest their truth
savoring your essence as
our enigmatic poetry.

Mirrored Amusement

You found me one sunstruck day
mirroring our minds
we spoke of past lives
so similar yet apart.

You were amused at my thinking
because you're intrigued
yet by nightfall
you believed in me.

I can't see or touch you
yet I play these words
as a song for you
so you can find my heart.

Memories

I found my place
awash on your shore
my mind numb
your voice, my light.
Waves took me then
onto rocks protecting you
fated memories I cannot lose.
I found my way
following your stream
sunlight in your eyes
as I sailed again
across starscaped skies
back to yours
memories I'll never lose.

Into the Night

I wait for you
trusting myself
against all nights
we've known before
as you wanted me; as I had you
we walked wild shores
against their tides
your brilliant madness
my maddening crazy
a fire upon our deep.
We're older this time
still sharing our empathic bond
crushing the unbearable light
wondering if we can heal us
before we go back into our night?

Fabled Dreams

We've always been adrift
throughout time
lost inside
our fabled dreams.

Shocked awoken I weep
your memory slipping away
my only remaining grasp
your lost metaphoric vision.

Yet you return each night
mapping my future selves
teaching me your way home
your sad eyes so patient.

Lonely Vineyards

You don't need to see
vintages of our taste
future planted seedlings
generations still waiting.

Yet the glass finds our lips
remembering sweet
lonely vineyards
so hopeful coming of age.

I love our waking game
patient as you find yourself
our twinned history
still making us up.

Thirty-sixing You

I remember the day
we forgot time
hours fell in love with minutes
we flew into our happy.

Who knew we'd still be here
kissing candles goodnight
again as we november us
thirty-sixing your beautiful.

Such is our fate
we remember everything
when we dream of us
time unwraps our laughter.

Anchoring Us

We play here to find us
our crazy eyes in love
songs we write
our only way home.

You knew me forever
an anchor you loved
we never touched shore
our only way home.

I finally understand you
both of us lost at sea
these siren calls for us
our only way home.

Chosen Words

Year's been one we waited
sharing light
your fires found me
burning my light inside out.

We love to speak in music
sharing your brilliant mind
searing language like
our hearts we've embraced.

So take my chosen words
find my enchanting song
remember our forty-fives
minutes that still burn.

Singing Our Calliope

Pages hold our lives
Written like stars across skies
Time finds your insight
Singing our Calliope
A light to find our way here.

Tasting New Light

Morning dawns our kiss
released of night's dreams
we wrap reverie inside
like your eyes in mine.

Sunlit rush awakens us
mounting our day
stories we've always written
under your gorgeous skies.

Tasting new light we play
keeping darkness bound
reflecting we're still
children of our sun.

Conjured Words

Ardently we think of you
wondering at your light
your words keys we find
opening perception's door.

It's a silent metamorphosis
written across my eyes
as I conjure up these words
strewn like paint upon my mind.

We find purpose hidden
behind longing eyes
such is our light we find
when we read yours.

Baking Revelations

We write our souls to poems
harvesting minds
patience finds us alone
searching for yours.

You move me in ways
words kiss my deepness
taking you inside
baking our revelations.

Precious light you share
such eyes binding love
no matter my final ashes
your memory makes mine real.

Lonely Sandcastles

Walking along our shores
naked toes sanding delight
wondering if my waves
found yours today.

High tide erases our steps
you got used to them
building lonely sandcastles
remembering ghosts.

Whispering softly in your ear
oceans crawl to your bed
song of ourselves
crash on us tonite.

BB King' ing Your Love

Write me in your daytripping
erase my yesterdays
taste my words tonight
help make my wings fly.

BB King your love here
let me sing your song
stand alone with me
hold my words in yours.

Remind me if I'm lost
we are so very alone
coldness tightens around us
let my wings hold you.

Passion Play

We sandcastle our happy
architecting beaches
while oceans storm relentlessly
astonishing shocked smiles.

Brilliant starlight bakes us
sanding our toes naked
we sing of our electric
a passion play in waves.

Screaming of delightful
you tackle my wanting
splashing your cool
we dive over our heads.

Tears Remember

Lost myself as snow fell
your eyes beaming inside me
all our storms weathered
now frozen memories.

Another year has stolen us
mirroring our steps here
" I'm scared" you cried
and then you were gone.

You never said goodbye
as fire and ice made us
so only tears remember
when love found us.

Lyrical Mind

Will you write about me
standing on the moon
your breath frozen crystals
like snow we played upon?

I remember snowflakes
tasting your looking
we'd laugh so cold
no one looked like you.

Winter has stolen you
these days alone we stay
your brilliant lyrical mind
my only road back to you.

Abandoned Smiles

You found me enigmatic
singing your song of us
my apprehension frozen
till your words found mine.

Yet year's chill stole us
our tears unchecked
as we knew not who we were
or wanted us to become.

Weeks have lost their way
our smiles abandoned
that look in our eyes
we've never shared.

Poignant Nights

We are lost without you
such music you sing
our dances under moonlight
always found me wanting.

You know my way home
your touch discovers
our words rewrote us
upon such poignant nights.

You found me writing
my song about you
dancing across today's words
such music we still sing.

Delirium's Breath

Your fire consumed us
sculpting our au revoirs
sipping delirium's breath
our frozen thoughts set free.

Can you still remember them
standing on your moon
letting time defy our
waves without a shore.

Intoxicated by flames
our minds race back
so alone lost drifting
in love's deepest tides.

Fading Dreams

Dawn's chill still reminds
we rode with no one else
even as the dream began
I'll never let you go.

Dazzling brown-eyed Calliope
you knew from the start
even as the dream fades
we'd never let us go.

As the darkness touches
I'll still sing of you
even as we dream again
will you let me go?

Unwrapping Tomorrow

In a year no longer roaming
safe inside our minds
we christmas lost time
wrapping up memories.

I would open them for you
gazing on your happy
sharing magic you sing
your beautiful heart.

Will you holiday your song
rainbow love to me
unwrap tomorrow together
help us all run free?

Saudade

Baking Yesterday

Where do we touch today
remembering looking back
all those nights alone
when we found our way?

Take me back in time
tell me your story again
follow my eyes inside yours
photograph my mind.

Holding you here on me
our singular moment
keeping time precious
when we baked yesterday.

Saudade's Storm

Riding a new wave
empty thoughts storm
as your words tomorrow me
haunted dreams wake us.

Little angels sharpen my take
creatures of our light
like a temple inside yours
sharing our saudade.

Retrouvailles took me
she demurred my attempts
knew you'd be watching
stimulating my storm.

Visions

Caught in canyon's surreal
when a day meant more
perhaps I'll find my way out
daydreaming of you.

Visions of a cloudless sky
when laughter ran ahead
we'd make us up again
baking time together.

So we climbed to tomorrow
leaving who we were
you never wanted more
daydreaming of us.

Storm's Tide

Rain loves sweet tears
kissing joy delightful
we measure our crazy
storms tide us together.

You take hold of me
wanting what you own
even my breath in yours
won't stop you making us.

I ride your words tonight
drenched in our laughter
we hurricane moments
storming into tomorrow.

A Room of Your Own

I remember the day you
moved into my mind.
A room of your own
inside my memories.

Do you still keep mine
as you peer out smiling
when you find these words
remembering you?

The days still find us
thinking alike as we write
of things we once knew yet
I wonder am I still inside yours?

Baking Our Delicious

Wrote you in my dream
words you used on me
making us live forever
when we loved everything.

Dancing in your light
those things you say
they fade by dawn
when you look at me.

You move holding my crazy
these words falling around us
like embers from our flames
baking our delicious.

Broken Leaves

Falling like broken leaves
atmospheres careen
you touch down on mine
windowing our light.

Open your eyes on me
should we know us
even as I'm let go
we'll never let it be.

Freedom paints our desert
sandstorms steal what's left
television asks if it's us
will you ever know me again?

Sand Dragons

Sand dragons sing moonlight
catching your magic
like how you found me
when night slipped into now.

I remember your lyrical
wandering through me
songs only we sing
once upon a lifetime ago.

Your painted landscapes
dawn cries all alone
calling out our names
when we finally remember.

Lost In Your Thoughts

Words make us up today
enveloping our minds
in dreams we play upon
rewriting us by dawn.

Where do I find us
lost inside such thoughts
gazing into yours
your magic binding mine.

You know you own me
your touch never stops
crazy fires shore our eyes
rewriting us over again.

Deserted Streets

Now your look reminds me
those days we first met eons ago
tangible electricity between us
gravity we never escape.

Fleeting yesterdays still hold
you knew we'd meet again
I'm the one waking here
our past lives collapsing into today's.

When we walk alone
even streetlights deserted
glances our only companion
your gravity keeps me sane.

Melancholic Atmospheres

Our melancholic atmosphere
seeps into these spaces
tries to erase my words
as you save them yet again.

I remember your first time
alone I flew these skies
terrified silence held me
no recourse for any calm.

Trapped inside reeling days
you found my lost mind
like touching someone in time
no one made me like you.

Autumn Ghosts

I'm sailing in a clouded sky
time traveling to find
all you left behind
ghosts that still say your name.

You knew I'd find them
as autumn leaves drop
and bare trees whisper
over these fluted notes you played.

Yet they've finally faded,
reminding me now
I'm just a glimmer in your
haunting memory.

Orpheus's Muse

You look deeper into me
than anyone I've known
and the thing is, love
your eyes never stop.

Orpheus's muse still sings
holding us in the dark
as we dream of dawn
when the light uncovers us.

When distant realms lure
hold your breath longer
and as the stars leave us
find mine looking back.

Planting Flowers

Plant your flowers in my eyes
hold my glance inside
your hands find me
make us want to stay.

You who seem to dream
what we thought we are
I know you so deep
taking me we fall into...

Losing it we run away
I knew we were lost again
our looks never stopped
sharing words we love.

Sharing Your Beautiful

Your rain falls like empty words
playing on my mind
they find frozen tears
hiding beneath struggling eyes.

Dewdrops misting morning's gaze
embrace memory's sorrow
caught by her swift undertow
I'm drowning inside yours.

Heartbroken left weeping for you
you're still by my side
holding my sad hands
sharing your beautiful.

Haunting Deepness

Walking in astonished light
we laugh it off sunglassing
it begs for our time
like when we first met.

I know how to find
what you tried to say
lost words in your eyes
mine blinded speechless.

Deep love haunts in silence
repaving yesterday
forgetting our way
light favors our shadows.

Ancient Tales

...to bind our dénouement
my days now chrysanthemum
poignantly remembering why
we storied so long together.

These words wrote us
singing passion plays
our shared muse delight
replaying an ancient tale.

We septembered hellos
drifting into sweet fires
a darkness survived yet
I have come to...

Streetlighting Dreams

Singing to me in a dream
I hear your lines take me
into your life at night
you didn't know I could.

Waking to drink them in
confused moments find us
shocked you awaken
but I'm already gone.

Were we really dancing
our words streetlighting us
songs in you singing of
hearts lost in this dream.

Making It Real

I remember not knowing
your smile, my thoughts
such a long time ago
when you were a dream.

We made it real as
lonely days found us fading
our minds sick thinking
of these lost words.

You won't forget me, love
when a new year takes us
the long road ahead
leading back to your heart?

Mystery Sail

Borne before the stars
her light found our dark
dancing in those eyes
capturing all of ours.

When she sailed away
we lost part of our soul
rocking with her gypsy
she sojourns before us.

Stars still smile for her
children growing love
making our universe
sail into her mysteries.

When Stars Fell

She's a secret in our hearts
never meant to be yet
touched our souls
when stars fell one day.

They sang of her blue light
such eyes became us
gazing our beautiful
love her only glimpse.

Such treasure beheld
no keys could keep her
evening's of blue sweet
we kissed her love farewell.

Trading Electricity

Why does my light flee
when you look away
left with my dark sun
I got used to yours.

We would trade electricity
bewitching our words
laughing like no one mattered
until we lost our way.

You haunted my mind
leaving just empty rooms
memories of our crazy
fading like love abandoned.

Finding My Soul

I sold my soul to yours
waiting under the sun
burnt and remembering
our timeless fire
shared as we laughed
astonished in our unique light
we'll always covet.

Without you now
I'll wait for the rain
hiding crazy tears
to find my soul again
singing your music
while I wonder
if you'll ever return.

Verde Mar Waves

Verde mar waves
take your embrace
awash in poetic eyes
we cross these lonely seas.

How did you feel leaving
we're both shattered
yet love remembers
sailing in yesterday's light.

I taste your mind in mine
alluring sweet darkness
we'd cast nets together
learning our new language.

Visions of Intuition

If you want you can find me
cloudcrofting mountaintops
eyes alone tearing
waiting for yours.

Snowpack debris recalls
we played gravity
chasing slippery slopes
our breathless kisses.

Glimmering atmospheres
painted our ghosts electric
such visions of intuition
walk me back to you.

Cryptical Magic

Stay to feel these words
of lives I ve painted
your beautiful mind my brush
mine a willing canvas.

Paint me in your songbook
make my real yours
our muses always laughing
whispering ourselves true.

Remember mine sweet
tempering our fires
love songs shared
alluring cryptical magic.

Our Waves

Silent beautiful your eyes
gazes of gorgeous shadow
slip into my open sky
like fragile ocean waves.

Storms distant we dance
steps brazen our thoughts
treasuring a glance
we ghost our way home.

Moonlit mountains beckon
our painted desert
your last look cries
a wave without a shore.

Childhood's End

We roam our memories
ebbing away from us
these days birthed alone
anchoring unfamiliar time.

She smiles inside a dream
knew our dear souls before
brought us here in light
embracing us with her love.

We sing our days together
laughing to play here again
this universe a sandbox
for our childhood's end.

Pillowing Tomorrow

Words are only streetlights
we walk our own way
touching yours here
my sweet reassurance.

If you want to read me
this is where I live sweet
making you up tonight
blanketing my dreams.

When you leave me
remember our laughter
these nights without you
pillowing tomorrow.

Touching Minds

Touching my mind yours
all our days inside words
we trade like lunar phases
measuring comprehension.

So we play imaginary solos
mapping linguistical scripts
making up our minds
as evening paints us closer.

Laughing you render me whole
eliciting my own dawning view
you knew I'd find you
touching your mind mine.

Freefalling

Gravity finds you closer
making me make you
wanting your sweet songs
you know I understand.

How do we keep singing
crazy days apart
you knew me right away
remembering my first words.

On a deserted shore
these words play us
waiting for another spark
freefalling into each other.

Crushing Saudade

Your vibe blankets me
words fall on my crazy
playing what we want
seeping into our now.

Like we've measured today
saving what we lost
our saudabe crushes
tears fallen to our song.

As your saxophone speaks
what we've played before
can I wrap my wings around you
freefall into our night?

Blanketing Desire

Walking into your sunset
we measure our laughter
like guitar riffs we love
playing with our yesterdays.

They crowd into our eyes
as skies paint tonight
new music finds us
blanketing desire.

Wicked smiles appear
your eyes laughing again
tempting mine to act
playing with our night.

Lost Tomorrows

Eerie quiet streets follow me
calling your name here
broken days find us
staring at lost tomorrows.

When the night sleeps
we fly together dreaming
all our words paint us
into the light.

Now you think of me
alone like your thoughts
I want to make them with you
walk our streets again.

Reconstructing Us

Pieces of you strewn here
like dunes of highway sand
they move with the wind
mindfully making you real.

What does touching mean
a race we never finish
and as the wind sighs
you move all around me.

Sudden saudade chill kisses
why do I remember you
lost signs smile a way
as you take me apart again.

Deep Roots

Your laugh measures us
in time with delight
every note holds my breath
as your glance captures me.

I remember our first dance
September's kiss
she knew our ways
sharing her laughter.

Our look changes like leaves
waiting till we know
a love we never let go
wintering our deep roots.

Forlorn Debris

Snowfallen glances breathe
glistening as we look
our cold sun bereft
a hope we forever.

Streets line our desperate
they sing like sighs
freezing our goodbyes
as we tempt what's left.

Lost amidst such debris
love puzzles us together
a fire we're drawn to
lighting up what remains.

Our Gravity

Will you hear my whispers
sighing with your gentle
as starlight falls
tempting who we've become.

Ocean waves ripple us
a shore we've always made
even as time ebbs away
your gravity embraces me.

We collide like sandstorms
as I find surprising moments
of your whispered poetry
dancing all over us.

Living with Ghosts

Clouds touch my tears above you
moments real only we know
living with your ghosts
terrified you're lost again.

Words I've shared
treasuring my only way
as long as love is
yours are always mine.

So we run away to find us
hiding behind our haunted
we're everything we know
your laughter sees my real.

Deepness Distilled

I was an unopened bottle
aging for your first taste
as time embraced me
my patience longed for you.

You kept me laughing then
sharing other's love
a deepness distilled
waiting till I came of age for you.

Gardens flourished within us
seeds of what we'd become
till one day you found me
as I opened up for you.

Dancing Eyes

Miles played our tables
mesmerizing aural metaphors
their rapt melodies surround
even your eyes danced.

Adrianne stole my heart
she sings my words of you
drowning heartbreaking waves
emotional melancholic enigmas.

And you like my silly songs
as we wade onto your shore
sinking deeper with each step
a dance we'll never forget.

Playing Us Again

Slipping into our moment
you crash my eyes
heartbreakingly gorgeous
taking all of me away.

Words trip over themselves
craving for a glimpse
they stumble from my mind
rewriting who I've become.

Laughter draws you here
my sudden adolescence
recalls our first time
replaying us again.

Sunburnt Time

Your eyes told me more
than I thought you'd say
as our music introduced us
so we talked after all.

We danced with the lyrics
ahead of our fleeting thoughts
your mind leading me
mine thinking ahead.

But the song ended
and you took those
gentle eyes away
leaving mine to say goodbye.

We met again eons later
recognizing our song
you found me first
gorgeous eyes you wield.

Sunburnt time still waits
our viral language
it's surreptitious dance
deciding what we think.

Socrates introduced us
knowing we could sing
shall we dance again, love
kiss my eyes with yours?

Glass Moments

Glass moments shatter time
haunting our dreams
we walk them home
photographing our surprise.

Memories of their footprints
wallpaper our minds
stepping into tomorrow
I've forgotten my way.

Your eyes plead for mine
will we ever really know
time's keys unlock us
as we go on our way.

Sipping Tomorrow

Her shadows follow me
teasing their aftertaste
my frantic footprints
lost but for another sip.

Visions of musing's crazy
open up my words
gonna find her moonlight
make our night shine.

We sauntered darkness
our eyes still glimmering
drunk on who we've become

sipping on tomorrow.

Gardening Love

Your happy dances like rain
kissing my face
my eyes summertime yours
gardening love.

Gorgeous ladybugs laugh
singing your delicious name
even lush forests know
trees stand to hold you.

Flowers stretch red petals
yearning for a touch
such alluring delight
spilling your beautiful.

Sandcastled Moments

Bopping around I've seen you
spilling smiles like champagne
all over my surprise
even your demure peeks out.

Laughing we find today
footprints wander just behind us
mingling on each other
they know where we're going.

Sandcastling our moments
time crashes around us
as nothing else is real
even my surprise is yours.

Painting Our Universe

I made a painting just for you
a child eyes in wonder
she found mine following
and her smile was my universe.

Lollipops and ice cream days
summer's laughter and
building winter's snowmen
spring's forever frozen love.

Held inside crushing tears
we look for her eyes here
she's everywhere now
I made a painting just for her.

Sympathetic Symphony

Days blur the meaning of us
prisoners of lost time
like a melancholic song
we can never let go.

Caught in our heavy tide
we struggle to understand
even words find new breath
when you touch my heart.

Of all of these moments
weaving a life within
we stay to find us
our sympathetic symphony.

Sequoyah & Nepenthe

Sequoyah stoked the fire's ash
morning dew spider webbing
as sunrise warmed the sky
gauntlet's challenge awaits.

Nepenthe sears her glance
winds violin the coming vibe
our tribe collects a hush
an eerie moon refuses to set.

We walk out under incredible
mountain thunder falls around
children's laughter sings
as we take the new day.

Gravity's Embrace

Stunned light remembers
an embrace we can't forget
yet you wonder
mesmerized by yesterday.

Etched on time's sand
your memory
photographs steal me back
one last look to find us.

Recollections bind my heart
even as our shore fades
like gravity letting go
even light tries to hold on.

Fire Dragons

Seemingly alone light wanders
remembering us
a luminous moment saved
because we became it.

Memories of lost love songs
wrapped us together
do you still keep that day
a fire upon our deep?

Chills play upon my heart
even as flames consume
we knew our dragon lived
soaring in our light.

Coyotes

Coffee shop scents shy off
our eyes hold hands
a last waltz before rain
we always played hearts.

Coyotes measure us all night
roads hold our canopy of light
till we're obliging prisoners
laughing with your best.

Masked we carnival delight
smoking our highway songs
nothing like a dead show
even Joni sang along.

Mesmerizing Change

Change takes you uninterrupted
slipping her arms in yours
before you realize
she's inside you playing.

When you laugh her away
as if we'd never go
even infinity loves her
crushing my saudade.

Do your eyes still dance
remembering her touch
mirroring now
she plays both sides of us.

Leaving Saudade

Saudade leaves frozen memories
they're scattered inside me
every room is full of them
but all the doors are locked.

We always shared a secret
a way to find us in the dark
when everything else fails
she would show us how.

Waves of nostalgia torment
like the look in your eyes
only a nuclear winter shows
how we find our way back.

Retrouvailles

The Game

I saw that look you found on me,
your tousled hair
checking out your lips
as you wrapped me around your finger.

You laughed when my voice decided
to play the game
our eyes knew was
already decided.

So we touched just
to check our sighs
before the winner
finally earned that kiss.

Melancholic Retrouvailles

You never knew who I was
shadows on your shore
like our first day
a lonely piano played us.

So we drift into sunlight
cherished glances evaporate
wondering who we're now
was anything ever real?

We both hold on
melancholic retrouvailles
our heartfelt dance
songs only we recognize.

Gossamers

Ghostlike touches find you
of my mind letting go
songs freed from our lips
gossamers of us

Silhouettes dance
threading memories
together like fingers
or your eyes on mine

Lucid drama unfolds on wings
nightfall's promised vision
of ancient days dreaming
when we could see us then.

Kissing Night

Her heart holds tales
of broken lovers
woven upon time's gift
gazing back at us.

Such is her beauty
finding ours in darkness
as we struggle today
lifted by her love.

She paints us here
under her gorgeous
sunsetting our pain
as we kiss the night.

Abandoned Smiles

You found me enigmatic
these questions of
my crazy apprehension
for your smile to stay.

We left the night cold
our wine untouched
as we knew not who
we really wanted to be.

So where are we now
as the smiles have gone
the crazy is despair and
our eyes have never seen?

Searing Moments

On wind under our sails
even smiles take root
voices court us now
a dance only you teach.

Delirium steps up its embrace
your kiss everyones me
delicious time moments you
lonely guitars play us.

Drumming heartfelt beats
days finally catch you
my searing touch
a dance only we learn.

Making Us Up

We used to share moments
electric visions of today
such maps we made
deserted starscaped shores.

They stole our hearts
laughing we found us
singing sweet tankas
making us up again.

We know we're outside time
love we've never lost
will you remember me on
days I'm lost without you?

Retrouvailles' Storm

What I find thinking of you
places we've been before
sandstorms my mind
as I breathe in all of you.

Walking inside your memory
sunlight kisses
flashbacks can't keep up
such is your deepness.

Wild retrouvailles reign
measuring desire
a lightness of being you
storms who I've become.

Bridging Your Shore

A separate reality we ask
uncertainty's questions
a timeless wish to share
light under your stars.

We burn just as bright
eyes aglow
bridging wilder shores
someday finding yours.

So we look to our hearts
such passion compels
our fires along this trek
yours still burns brightest.

Chrysalis's Fate

Like new skies today
everything about yours
when I take to mine
measures who we'll become.

Stepping through time
how we find ourselves
when uncertainty stays
chrysalis's rewrites us.

Your wings knew how
empty skies open for us
everything about desire
rapt within our retrouvailles.

Kissing January

January loved playing our real
she dances laughing
we cannot look away
her frost licking our lips.

Yet these frozen moments
copiously entwined
find both of us
snowfalling time.

Should we bury these thoughts
Taste our frozen memory
skating on her icy breath
as she makes us both real?

Pandemic's Blues

Our poetry finds us
beautiful eyes holding hands
across vast pandemic sighs
such is our only delight.

Sharing passionate dances
our words love to waltz
enrapturing happy
as we fall into our night.

Will you share your song
no matter where our
dreams dwell
as nightfall's frolic invites?

Mesmerizing Memories

Sipping your smiling wine
I fall into enchanted
Alice's wonderland
as you walk me there.

We caress our music
a dance that touches
sweet as you follow mine
daring me to make yours.

I take you back to me
our haunting soundtrack
mesmerizing memories
as we mirror each other.

Whispered Intent

I step onto your shore
apprehension licks my lips
you carry my eyes
whispering your intent.

Footprinting our lost way
we fall into our past
delighted to come home
stars hiding behind you.

You saunter into my mind
as another memory of us
provokes my words here
rendering me all yours.

Lessons

We move in light and dark
our minds sojourn back
replaying understanding
uncovering what we've missed.

Our real escapes everyone
mirrors picture our past
constructing our worlds
your lens captures us.

I knew you many times before
we locked memories away
as children we always return
another lifetime; another lesson.

Smoking Cubans

Turntabling Louis Armstrong
takes me back to you
smoking cubans we sang
laughing at all our curiosities.

You played me in tune
dancing with our mysteries
who knew we'd attach like
tillandsias holding court.

I remember your eyes on mine
mirroring my wanton intentions
Louis knew all along
we never stepped on toes.

Footprints In My Mind

Last night I forgot time
lingering in a snowstorm
yesterday's frozen moments
searing my mind cold.

How do we forget
crystalline days together
my snowscaped footprints
leading me back to you.

Without you now
I'm waiting for the sun
to help erase my memory
so I can find my way home.

Lyrical Wings

She knew how to dance
synesthesia taught her
a lyrical electric mind
such wings no one shares.

Bridging songs I never heard
days became gorgeous
we walked along similars
mesmerized by our bond.

Writing tomorrow's music
a dance no one has seen
my delight has taught me
it's never too late to fly.

Learning to Dance

We stepped into this world
our days surreptitiously
slipping past as
they showed us why.

We learned to dance
catching our breath
such was my thought
as you showed me why

We sang our lives together
sharing moments
we'll take them home
if you let me show you why.

You followed me here
how do we remember us
our time here fleeting away
days seducing what's real.

You knew I wanted you
catching our breath
such was our thought
as we considered tonight.

You laugh taking us
delicious'ing all of me
we sing ourselves again
there's always tomorrow.

Heisenberging Now

Waiting we skate into us
Heisenberging now
no one is real
masking intent like we do.

Tension sexual allures us
do we look deeper or dance
how can we make us up
no one knows if we're real.

You laugh taking me
measuring my dénouement
looking inside my mirror
unmasking tonight's desire.

Making Her Real

She preens her thoughts
they find her curious
will you know her way
to share them again?

Starlight alights within her eyes
a glimmer of your desire
as she considers you
puzzled if you'll pursue

She rewards you a glance, a sigh
reflecting on her beautiful
you know the way
will you make her real?

New Orleans Jazz

Friday's dusk reminds
even twitter disappears
your writing befriends you
sharing its dark hug.

Visions of electric bars
her eyes, your gravity
we took that dance
jazzing into New Orleans.

Evening's chill awakens
other ones you remember
such songs abandoned now
as you wait for hers.

Raining Electricity

Your pages turn as I find you
yesterdays thoughts
I will miss your gravity
painting our sky.

Even desert sand storms
as your electricity rains
playing our songs
and the words we left.

Lovers find us today
poets show how we know
our eyes such old friends
writing about our tomorrow.

Letting Her Fly

An angel appeared beside me
she slipped into my mind
My dear love, she said
You must let her fly.

Astonished I had a waking dream
we were walking hand-in-hand
so many times before
as we laughed under our sun.

Tears overcame me as she left
whispering like a goodbye kiss
She knows you love her
She will walk with you again.

Imaginary Guitar Solos

So as we turn off our music
imaginary guitar solos remain
they touch off new tears
evaporating our rapport.

The evening of our laughter
stills these trying times
as we bridge tonight
looking for who we once were.

Nothing tastes like yesterday
even our new songs cry for us
will you want to play again
build another fire?

Frozen Yesterdays

Your light around me sweet
composing us as we look
you taste my words
deciding if I'm yours.

Could've known you knew
even when we were alone
stealing another glance
wanting me to take yours.

How do we make crazy work
all our moments lost
like frozen yesterdays
still holding us together.

Sojourn

Spacetime birthed us here
our mother star
shares her light
this sojourn we caravanserai.

Darkness surrounds our trek
we live our days together
huddling close
keeping our faith in her.

These imaginary songs
they help me find my way
following your beautiful
my sisters and brothers.

Ghosting Smiles

Cerulean hues paint my dawn
blanketing lost dreams
I ride yesterday's echos
remembering who I am.

They thunder in my mind
recalling your storms
visions of future days alone
we knew they were coming.

Haunted eyes cannot escape
seeing your ghosted smile
like a lyrical voice
reminding me who you were.

Breathless Waves

Our eyes saxophone secrets
only the night can share
indulgent memories
as we make up new words.

We bridge strange suns
sharing ancient light
such is our dénouement
only to turn back time.

Patient tempo paints us
a dance we never stop
these breathless waves
overwhelming us again.

Surreal Storms

Your snowfall chills me
beautiful light touches us
left in our surreal storm
we play like children.

Gorgeous fascination overtakes
my imagination piqued
you laugh knowing me
no one else notices us.

Slipping beside myself I look
your eyes owning mine
even our music binds
my words finding yours.

Waves

Your electric runs through me
energy beyond mine
sensing your real
you balance our wave.

Nascent emotional current
holds my sudden thought
desire ripples over us
like an hypnotic touch.

Grounded against others
we throw caution away
insulated in a glance
another wave takes us away.

Broken Pieces

Days disappear yet I stay
walking inside my mind
searching empty rooms
where did we leave us?

My words still sing you
mirroring days between
shadows that took us
whispering who we were.

How will time find us now
lost inside our memories
will broken pieces of us
fit together again?

Ghosted

Demons stole childhood's end
thrust into another universe
we've always lost us
never knowing who we are.

Ghosted by haunted love
we sing lonely songs
only darkened skies see
how we found our way.

Turbulent waves take us
finding our real
love's true deepness
longing for our light.

Strange Days

Strange days find us all
We worry about our loves
They move us to tears
As nightfall blankets us now
Find your moment to hug them

Shadow Play

She plays in our minds
Skies her beautiful for us
When the sun touches
Thoughts reign wonder in her play
Held in shadows of the moon.

Island Shores

Sunlight streams through me
my human shape a lens
between galaxies and atoms
we share our water of life.

Suspended between such vast
how do we find ourselves
islands of our world
I'm afloat in search of yours.

Our shores filled with wonders
depths of joy we learn
will you find mine again someday
share your light with me?

Mesmerizing Dark

Morning recalls us here
her gentle thoughts lucent
lighting eyes together
for yesterday's promise

Daylight shadows me
echoing lost dreams
spring's dulcet rainstorms
reminds of past tears

Eventide washes today
refreshed stars awaken
mesmerizing our dance
we sing her silent song.

Viral Language

I'm looking for you
language a semiotical road
we take everything inside
remaking us.

It's how we play today
testing if we're real
do you really want mine
rewriting you again?

Our words combine within us
we're not who we seem
children still learning to be
speaking in our language.

Aphrodite

Goddess of the Moon

All of these words are
yours tonight.
Drink them with the
evening sky as it
plays above us,
opening a page for
seductive's mood,
singing to us,
as we watch
Othiym Lunarsa,
goddess of the moon
slip away and
embrace her lover as
she sets onto her stage
for us with a kiss.

Seduction's Muse

We met accidentally,
our eyes never settling
my words rushing you
yours tempting mine.

They seduced us both,
your mystery so alluring;
drinking wine together
they found love a muse.

But the scattered days
took them apart as our
stories drifted away and
we left this theater alone.

Sunglassing Me

Delight asks if you're real
reading my lips
she knows you so well
laughs at my inside joke.

Your eyes sunglass me
so you saunter into mine
we know why we're here
mirroring our smiles.

When you name me
you're all I want, sweet
fingers through your hair
as you taste my champagne.

Torrid Madness

Deep bass digs us under
heavy atmospheric rapport
electronic vibe lures
a torrid rave drowns.

Delirium beckons a dance
smoking smiles like a sigh
crazy eyes kiss reticent
sultry madness entrances.

Gravity introduces us
egos forget our names
a mesmerizing urge
no one leaves unknown.

Tantalizing Time

You whispered in my ear
do you want to play me
your cowgirl movie
tantalizes time to stop.

We linger in such ambient
making us up yet again
simmered in delicious
creme brûlée'ing now.

Soaking in our sauternes
lips drunk on your sweet
I hold my breath as you
take me into your own.

A Love Supreme

She dances with me
takes my hand & looks to me
such dreams I cannot stop
all that remains of her.

She knows I love her
happiness so rare it glitters
in her eyes, her mind
she loves all of us.

I love to dance with her
I take her hand, her eyes
a smile returned
she's everywhere.

Of light and love
of you, of us
empyreal delight in sacred time
reflections of us all.

Childhood's end awaits
of dreams we hold dear
alas, upon this shore
our searing beacon in life.

Another door awaits devotion
our deeper universe within
to truly be one with you
our love supreme.

Pas de Deux

Long notes make us
we saxophone a glance
willing fingers drum
our throbbing cadence.

Pianissimos's gentle steps
holds us in melody
finding adagio's time
for dawn's pas de deux.

Your rhythm carries us
sweet glittering sunlit smiles
making duet delicious
tasting our dolce in a kiss.

Tasting Your Light

Memories of you firefly
across my dark eyes
glancing back in time
streetlighting yesterday.

Dancing within your light
our nights awakened us
you loved to take my hand
make me touch your dark.

We'd find a shy dawn
whispering sweet songs
you'd make me then
tasting your light again.

Storms

Suddenly we're a storm,
crashing through doors
eyes and fingers crazy
zippers & buttons and us.

I make you again over
my touches, your gasps
these eyes on fire as
I take you through it.

You make me again
your kiss, mine back
our storm, our minds
we do not stop the rain.

Paradoxical Songs

Abandoned astonishment
my days now collide
seemingly innocent memory
telling yesterday tales.

Your words fragment me
deciphering today
such labyrinthine questions
my only recourse ahead.

Sanity's answers refused
I walk away shattered
your paradoxical songs
my only remaining touch.

Blue Shores

When nightfall kisses you
on that island paradise
we see your electric eyes
through our broken sighs.

Lamenting lovers adrift
oceans beyond sunsets
writing sad songs
sung on our blue shores.

Midnighting we roam afar
dreaming of a blues bar
holding tight under the light
of its neon moon.

Dolce's Kiss

Long notes take me tonight
saxophoning your look
fingers drum impatiently
do you still wonder too?

Pianissimos's gentle sweet
steps holds us in melody
finding adagio love
please sing with me.

Take us home baby
your bass beat makes
solo delicious on us
tasting our dolce in a kiss.

Simmering Thoughts

Whispering close to you
tears flood our beautiful
they secret my uncertainty
like rain on my lips.

Simmering thoughts make us
drinking our minds
wondering if that kiss
still wanted another.

I silence my poetic
dazzled by your look
wanting summer's breeze
drying our lonely tears.

Mesmerizing Slopes

Your music speaks to me
such visions I cannot share
so you take me again
eyes commanding me
gazing into my captured mind
saying you're all I want.

Lost I follow your lead
dancing across our smiles
down into mesmerizing slopes
wet from my lips
taking hold of our desire
we seal the night's stage.

Friday Me

You haunt my memories
no rooms are empty
my thoughts slaved to yours
across radioactive landscapes.

You find me wanting more
feeling alone you Friday me
our apocalyptic tastes
dripping from our words.

Break in to me baby
steal my thoughts tonight
dive deep me for
don't wake us up now.

Taking My Crazy

You make me feel this
everything I wanted in you
strange I'm gone now
inside these lost words.

You've had me on fire
alone dreaming of you
we knew you would walk
taking my crazy with you.

I think of you moving in
I could tell you were real
spending my time
because you owned me.

Moist & Delicious

Moist finds my touch
a song you make as
I move between your notes;
your eyes still singing mine.

Your rhythm moves mine
we follow and take a kiss,
another touch,
your ambrosial found.

Locked, your fingers, mine
a dance, this waltz,
you lead me to another find;
you're delicious.

Wanting Us

Saw you drinking last night
everyone staring too
sipping my favorite
cause you know I want some.

We dance thinking sex
your eyes holding me
your lips asking for mine
do you want another?

You make me touch you
naked in our minds
everything we wanted now
cause I know you want some.

Warming Up Her Happy

Her smile thaws your frost
as she skis grooming
your slippery slopes
waxing her delicious.

Carving heated runs
you slalom together
turning frozen tracks on fire
free-styling all night.

You traverse out-of-bounds
holding on to her wicked
schussing intents as
you warm up her happy.

Fever

Tasting her sweet dream
my thoughts poetic
surreptitiously they take
holding my mind prisoner.

Reminiscing her storms
like laughter in the rain
I lose myself in her
our music, my deepness.

Winter's grip still commands
as we plan our escape
diving back in time
bedazzled by fever.

Paradise Found

Surreptitiously my mind holds
your red smile beckons
exotic tastes, my lips, yours
caressing eyes approach.

We dance around intention
singing gorgeous art
stunned I inhale scent
you know I'm yours.

Such pleasures command
your paradise found
opening your rose
a taste like no other.

Tasting Words

I don't stay very long
my life is short like a
song caressing your lips
but the dance is sweet.

You love my language
tasting my words as
they roll off your tongue
waiting for their taste.

We match steps as my
thoughts become yours
singing us home
with your exquisite eyes.

Cascading Pleasures

Roaring music takes my breath
alive with your blues
waterfalling around us
into sunstruck light.

Moist eyes reminiscing
days of naked delight
we tempo it's song
fervently immersing our souls.

Light fades as we conjure
torrid dreams of abandon
as red daisies sing of
cascading pleasures.

Looking For Your Real

Surreal days accelerate
waking us in dreams
metaphors find gazes
longing for your words.

Glitterati's stone glance
hides lost eyes as
we walk crazy days
looking for everyone's real.

Nightfall dances seduce
beckoning gravity's lust
as summer liaisons horizon
our last goodbye kiss.

Morning Dew's Apéro

Dancing eyes drink your words
tasting sweet dulcet
our morning's dew apéro
delighted dawn embrace.

How does today find
passionate sentiments
such thoughts we write
hold coquettful smiles.

Delighted pauses consider
playing across your lips
should we voice such
words to enchant?

Climaxing Lavazza

Morning dew tastes my lips
your Arabian Sanani heat
tripping Jamaican Blue fantastic
we sheet ourselves for coffee

Barefooting on Kenyian wood
we kama sutra bodies
intelligentsia heats our minds
climaxing liquid lavazza

Awake we clothe the day
inhaling lingering fumes
galactic black, no sugar
we make our own.

Afternooning Dreams

Visions of you play across skies
sunrising my eyes
dawning with first light
passion awakening us again.

We afternoon our coyness
languishing onto these smiles
I puzzle you together here
imagining your strike look back.

Dusk finds us measuring
sunsets in your sweet sky
as you find me nightfalling
alone inside yours.

Distant Shores

Sighing interstellar winds reach
touching our eyes tonight
smiling as they alight
making yours all too real.

Such songs we play
whispering stars lure us
nightfalling into their charm
ohh but stay with me instead.

Lover's glimmering looks ask
why stray distant shores
dreaming of other lands
tempting our fates?

Chasing Our Words

Take my love in yours
find these eyes on you
when my words fail me
gift me yours instead.

If you want to see me
open your beautiful
sail those wings in my sky
fly with me tonight, baby.

When love found us here
you know it's intense
we've waited so patiently
chasing our words home.

Another Dance

You found me laughing
eyes dancing on mine
you led; I followed
steps we just made up.

Songs making my words
playing you as I wrote them
you'd look up at me
asking are we still right.

Glistening we would cool
so you laughed your happy
kissing mine goodbye
leaving for another dance.

Bound Lust

Blood drums up your passion
seething like bound lust
as you walk onstage strumming
even your eyes are on fire.

Meeting me halfway home
exhilaration crawls over us
begging for just one touch
into a song we dive deep.

Space guitars what remains
an eerie mesmerizing glow
your look begs my temptation
pleading for your release.

Abandoned Petulance

Petulant lips pleading
eyes follow my thoughts
dancing with her words
she knew mine would wane.

Pocketing her smirks
I move on our shared delight
over my lap she dances
smacking upon each pleasure.

Eyes plead for her peace
counting tarried strike
such petulance abandoned
her moans still rule our night.

Gardening Nights

Red flowers fill your mysterious eyes
landscaping my mind
like sunburst clouds
mountaineering your smile.

Walking into your song
you surreptitiously find my hands
making me yours
stealing my eyes.

Laughter blankets abandon
you know what you do
taking me again
gardening our night.

Nightfalling Crazy

I could write about you
these words we've shared
such light you have become
beyond my imagination.

You could write about me
songs lyrical you sing
such light we became
you knew me before I did.

We silent our words
nightfalling this crazy
dreaming of our real
wanting no one else.

Finding My Lost

Your deep dark knows my pain
when you lose your mind
will you remember me
before we go insane?

We wear our wild eyes
like fire diamonds aglow
weeping for love
holding on to sanity.

Beyond these words we pray
making love to stay here
can you find my lost
before you dance away?

Cherished Enigmas

Whimsical tastes penetrate
baking inside my mind
a dance we've scored
deepening trusted memories.

Singing electric now
we lingua franca today
dialecting our secrets
inventing cherished enigmas.

Washing ashore like bottles
we break open dawn
butterflying fervid embraces
euphorically making us up.

Commanding Distractions

She moves across shared skies
circling desire's intent
as lovers Jupiter & Saturn
finally kiss beyond her light.

Such night's embrace
caress our eyes
making out fantasies
upon Seychelle's heat.

Writing tomorrow's song
I play upon your mind
commanding distractions
everything for your night.

Riding Cowgirl

Cowboying my way with you
even my ride laughs
yet your eyes don't leave
shooting that song goodbye.

Will we burn sheets tonight
waiting till we taste us
if you want my blues
will you share yours?

Bound to a past we loved
making us up again
tried to hold your crazy
cowgirling your way with me.

Aphrodite's Smirk

Aphrodite's smirk delights
arousing tempestuous fire
laughter holds our spirit
caught in tides of light.

Lunar shine steals us
Desire wants to see
moonlit lips dance
even stars caress us.

Our ménage à trois unfolds
delicious on such a stage
each one makes demands
as we all submit again.

Rhapsodic Seduction

You coyly pastourelle my eyes
binding with that look
spanking my thoughts
taking me as I dare submit.

Provoking my interest
your naked heat arises
stripping with a laugh
you top me with your wet.

Obedient my submissive cry
begs for another
as these frenzical nights
flood our steamy dawn.

Hungry for you I reach
delicious my tongue owns
soaking your slopes
your moan binds mine.

Sunday's rhapsodic seduces
punishing my daring ask
wanting more you strike
blindfolded I am your command.

Moving into me you kiss
stroking my fire
lips dance across it
deeper into my submission.

Cowgirls

Wet lips set our pose
wine sauntering in us
bass notes beckon
I wonder where you've been.

Our driving beat envelopes
catching another wanting
an unknown cowgirl plays
reading my mind again.

Losing moments we catch up
your eyes lightning
another sip stirs
you've always been mine.

Coveting Vibes

Searing atmosphere binds
I feel your madness
strange vibes measure
caught between yours and mine.

Words saxophone your lips
moving all over mine
lashing an alluring dance
a poem we've always been.

Bound eyes slay restraint
they own our light
tied to what you want
coveting what I do.

Cascading Desires

Slipping inside I feel you
light cascades around us
your liquid eyes on fire
taking mine captive.

Our thoughts reign
your smile swims to me
electric touches enthrall
smoking our crazy.

Sunshine explodes all over you
dripping in my eyes
spellbound I'm yours
I know what you want.

Footprinting Your Beautiful

When you realize it's us
sailing across our vast
every beach you touch
footprints your beautiful.

Our words kiss to be
you've known me before
our shores beckoning
trying to figure us out.

Making us up every day
It's like you don't remember
strung out laughing
who we used to be.

Aftertastes

I could find you anywhere
our crazy making us up
you'd remind me laughing
every word we played.

Like a sip of delicious wine
our aftertaste remains
I'd write about your look
imagining who we could be.

These empty thoughts
caressing yours
poetry we wrap within
as evening takes us.

Canopies

Canopies of your beautiful
light who we were
like days we couldn't stop
laughter's echos.

I'm going to hold your song
sleepless across our eyes
nights we're dreaming
until you look back.

Even when our crazy sighs
who we wanted to be
will you still remember
when we're someone else.

Gifting Gazes

So we find ourselves alone
no one to read our lips
such is your beautiful
asking about mine.

A gaze you gift kisses
as we dance here
like when I first saw you
punishing my questions.

So we find us wanting
our laughter measuring
asking to touch minds
everything else falls away.

Losing Our Crazy

Waiting for you to see me
we made us painting words
laughing when they crashed
loving when they stopped.

We make us up each day
losing our crazy
rapping your beautiful
searching for mine.

Days abandon me
all these memories lost
like your eyes in my dark
waiting for me to see you.

Igniting Us

August shores against us
hot sand delights
stunned waves shock
igniting us again.

Scorching sunlit skies
blinded eyes lock
behind shadow's intent
laughing about everything.

Darkened clouds interlope
masking wicked lips
baby I know your way
nightfalling my shore.

Your Glance

The rain found us tonight
you wanted me then
storming against mine
no one takes me like you.

All night your look deep
saving mine like you knew I'd
find these words
tasting your glance.

Dawn breaks our hold
deliciously wrapping us up
you bury me under laughter
our music sunlighting us.

Playing on Vinyl

How did you know
skating around me
like you already decided
I was your song.

Your rhythm set me down
cueing your deep
like those albums we played
nothing else sounds like us.

Our soundscape envelopes
whispering sighs like the wind
our deep still crushing us now
replaying that moment.

Prisoners

Surreal touches down
we never really leave
it's just time keeps us
prisoners outside now.

Shall we make up stories
days when we were free
helpless within our fires
just so we know it's real.

You look past my words
searing moments gifted
stunned I unlock us so
we happen onto now.

Ocean & Cloud

Ocean and Cloud
went on a date tonight
holding yesterday's hands
as they made love.

Ocean loves Cloud
he follows her shadows
till moonlight fades her
gentle sunlit rain.

Cloud loves Ocean
she gifts him glances
foreshadowing her ephemeral
before raining her love.

Cloud wakes sisters
Mist and Fog
as bored with Ocean's waves
she touches Land.

Land needs Cloud
knowing brother Ocean found her
so he dries her tears
as her sisters weep over him.

Ocean storms Land
looking for Cloud
flooding him with cold as sister
Wind kisses them to sleep

Ocean dawns with Sun's
love filled with happy,
yet sad as Cloud is gone
and Sky is blue with grief.

Ocean builds stairways
climbing to Sky, hoping
to see Cloud before Sun
fades with his happy.

Cloud plays with Land
as Sun sees them hiding
Shadow he made to
help Ocean find her.

Sky covers us in stars as
Evening surreptitiously wanes
our mood taking Sun,
leaving Moon lighting our way.

Does Night find you curious
as you peer across starscapes
remembering Day
and lover's kiss?

Dawn chills, gently touching
what's found overnight,
and we ask
is love Light?

Apprivoisément

Apprivoising Wildness

Her flawsome intoxicates
torrid saudade imprisons
as haunted ghosts bind
she laughs and kisses me.

Sighing winds forget-me-not
who we used to be
when time baked us
into words you would sing.

To apprivoisé your wildness
stars would bend light
empty thoughts would flee
and I would fly to you.

Samba & Waltz

You knew me in moments
we've never met before
without finding words
we fell into our minds

Yours is the samba
a sweeping tour de force
we cannot stop our eyes
on yours, or yours in mine

Mine is the waltz
a silent dance we make
moving to find our words
for tonight's caravanserai.

Butterflies

You turned on me,
moving so quickly
time forgot to tell me to be
and I lost myself.

We carried your days,
my nights as your sunlight
shadowed mine and
I rushed to find my say.

Alas, your wings took hold
as startled I stopped
my lips barely in motion
but I can't speak butterfly.

Time Streams

No one walks these streets
carving paths only I see
time skips just ahead
I lose my way catching up.

We run in different spaces
your time measures mine
laughing we play these games
never quite in sync.

I try to stop time remembering
as yours streams by mine
carving your own future
my own just out of reach.

Footprints

I'll always remember you
lost within your ocean
my mind shoring yours
sharing waves we made.

I know what you felt then
days we took laughing
how could we forget
there was no one like us.

You know how I felt too
your mind's fire in mine
soft-voiced footprints
leading back to who we were.

Painting Time in Music

Sanguine ladybugs garden her mind
gorgeous dancing creatures
child-like wonder finds a smile
sharing time in our box of rain.

Carmine light shadows footprints
her lyrical laughter follows them
they rise and fall captivated
as an unheard song is born.

Damasked flowers yearn a touch
painting time in music
patterns fill our worlds
gifts only her synesthesia opens.

Haunted Smiles

You found me walking alone
as we wrote in our thoughts
when I turned to say hello
you shared that haunted smile.

We stopped our time then
touches kept us here
momentarily together
wrapping up our words.

I'd been waiting for you
time laughing back at me
as you flashed your magic
haunting my smile as well.

Electric Eyes

Starlight takes me home
bathed in sweet memories
a rain of poetic eyes
gently whispering your name.

Feels like you've always known
Selene blushes as she sets
waking our night alive
peeking back at your happy.

Sol beckons us to dance
as you take my hand again
such exquisite electric eyes
kissing mine home.

Shadows on Sand

Your fire saunters on sand
shadows become mesmerized
we wrap sunlight over us
chilled eyes bask on desire.

Searing looks bake us
mapping sunstruck smiles
you gift my moment
as clouds hurry over.

Cooling temperament rules
our fingers say hello
dripping with relief
we sandcastle delight.

Saxophoning Our Real

Your sound captivates me
circling within my mind
you mesmerize everyone
no drumz knows your beat.

Furious tempo takes us
as we rhythm together
laughing like no one
saxophoning our real.

How do we find us now
symphonies moment what was
as we step across space
your eyes finding time in mine.

Ghosts

So cold dawn still stays away
ghosting me
like a cloud in a storm
hiding inside her rain.

Oh I know she loves me
eyes that make you real
even in our searing light
I see hers baking mine.

Night cools desert streets
asking if I know my way
when no one remembers
only my ghosts are real.

Silent Arpeggios

Thoughts glissando within me
tearing through my days
memories of your eyes
holding mine inviolate.

Yesterday imprisons me
leaving sacrosanct chants
time's silent arpeggios
all that I know now.

Dawn razes your apparition
leaving me alone again
weeping piano keys
are all that remain.

Drinking Songs Like Wine

Your songs made love to me
got drunk on their words
even time left me faded
holding on to them.

Ballads story our lives
weaving your colors
visions we'd sing
sharing our beautiful.

I'd write about you every day
painting in your sky
we'd drink songs like wine
kissing time goodbye.

Rising Tides of Light

Sultry bodies miraging eyes
desert heat soars
sizzling conversation
swimming in pools of light.

Smoking on our skin
delicious ripples deepen
inviting sensuous
we soar in sky's canyons.

Rising tides of light beckon
playing on our shores
scenes we'd replay again
baking new memories.

Emotional Thunderstorms

Touching a dark place
no one sees the harm
it's so cold deep inside
even sunlight withers away.

Memories abuse our past
thoughts abandon reason
deserted we were all alone
inside emotional thunderstorms.

Sunlit rainbows seek me out
even when you hello
you're all I wait for now
lighting up my mind.

Cloudscapes

Mountain cloudscapes sky us
inviting empyreal visions
rising around desert heat
they catch our breath.

Beyond my space
you share a deeper look
I'm bound to our play
becoming yours.

So I climb day's light
struck by your vision
clouds melt into stars
as we fall into night.

Fading Into You

When heat made us crazy
we'd vibe till dawn
sultry smiles kissing the sun
till our laughter came home.

Trying on my eyes
you'd fade into me
as the moon peeked in
daring us to come out.

I'd play my words for you
songs no one else hears
you'll remember them someday
when your smile catches mine.

Desire's Intent

I met you septembering me
trying on my smile
days we wrote fire
trees changed clothes.

Makes me want to take you
walk our past home
slipping on what we knew
like pajamas know silk.

So we leave desire's intent
strewn like fallen leaves
each one tells a story
sunsetting on who we were.

Galactic Caravanserai

Strange sunlight kisses you awake
distant realms stream inside
alien shores beckon for footprints
on beaches from neighboring stars.

You walk from room to room
windows open to exotic scenes
time has lost its way as
worlds doorstep for your play.

Caravanserai'ing galactic arms
we dwell upon distant joys
delectable menus crowd around
pleading us to taste their charms.

Haunted Butterflies

Château d'Yquem on your lips
I follow her comfortable sip
laughter measures us
even as you're gone.

Butterflies take me over
haunting your words
goodbyes encrypt me
rewriting what's left.

Whispers steal my soul
no one plays us like you
nightfall forgets me
remembering your taste.

Beautiful Storms

Shared smiles find us
writing stories we treasure
in this searing light
even our storms become words
as we measure beautiful.

Gravity's Wake

As the days beckon
such is their light around us
as the nightfall hugs
gravity's wake immerses
only time keeps us apart.

As darkness descends
even light sends her first touch
waking what we'd see
atoms colliding within
guiding what we're in search of.

Wrapping Us Poetic

We made our own road
caravanserai'ing us
days wondered in joy
each dance rewrote what was real
wrapping poetry in us.

Yesterday's Poetry

Time gates us so we know
you and I are here to dance
our words map today
to yesterday's poetry.

Each glance you fire
tears space like gravity holds
taking my words
against what you gift.

So we've stepped in time
mesmerized by our samba
learning to be us
caught in tomorrow's wake.

Clouded Silhouettes

She stepped out into my sun
shadows crowd behind us
chasing her superstar
even desert clouds shy away.

Photographing laughter
scenes only lovers make
when night was ours
playing lines we owned.

Days streak across our sky
stories we won't stop
making us up
like clouded silhouettes.

Fallen Moondust

She is of moondust fallen
deftly on your soul
like mirrored light
caught in your eyes.

Footprints find you
gazing at what might be
like her inviting eyes
holding your breath.

Wanting familiar you look
across her subtlety
asking desire's intent
captive in her eternal.

Becoming Us

Rain-glued memories
windowpane my mind
framing these thoughts
to storm with yours.

Such is our design
as we replay yesterday's joy
reaching for what was
hoping what might be.

Prism'ed light finds us
as we reflect again
painting us over
calming what we've become.

Strange Music

Dripping onto wary footprints
my bloodline abandons me
streetlights blink in horror
forgetting my blindness.

Wanton thoughts scour me
her sticky blade hugs deep
black eyes torment
tricking my treat.

She laughs as I crash
her heels kiss me
strange music plays
eclipsing my farewell.

Allure's Masquerade

I could write about you
we've always met
masquerading allure's smile
knowing yours tastes sweet.

We moment stolen glances
our gambit refreshing
should you move against me
will I stay if you do not?

Your clock dominates me
as we chess our lives
do you want me here
unmasking yours?

Queen's Fate

You wait for my move
gambiting your desire
our eyes electric shocks
every look we share.

How do we reconcile today
we take our words to bed
writing our intentions
across crazy abandon.

Laughter sips on your lips
wakes these sad eyes
I hold your Queen's fate
as you checkmate mine.

Blanket of Stars

Take my hand and
follow my eyes as we
play you in the new day
a song like no other.

Your gravity becomes mine
and we laugh at our play
tantalizing each other
under the blanket of stars.

Our night becomes us again
glittering laughter, your eyes
my smile, so we touch
as the stars look on.

Lost Words

You went away one day
taking us with you
I don't know who you left
but whose words are these?

I remember being me
making these lines with you
your sad smile drifting
secretly showing me you.

You held my hand that day
knowing these days gone
I'd lose everything
becoming who you saw.

Yesterday's Universe

Distracted I wander thru
memories looking for you
wanting them to embrace
but they've slipped away.

Suddenly alone I forget
my way back, my mind
full of doors and rooms
but no one lets me in.

Who do we talk to when
yesterday's universe
no longer needs us and
today's can't remember?

New Light

We all go alone into night
your touch my beautiful
it keeps us sane
holding us in your eyes.

Confused moments tell us
we are like you too
our stories unfolding
making up what we dream.

Do we find morning's real
tasting new light washing over us
true enough to shine yet
keeping our words real?

Shall We?

Saw your moonlit dance
alluring rhapsodic moves
lost in your thoughts
cause you know I want some.

We talk forgetful words
my eyes holding yours
your lips asking mine
shall we, you and I?

Your reach seduces me
undressing my mind
naked thoughts frame us
cause I know you want some.

Fragile Memories

Can you make me real
sail my turbulent sea
surf these waves
find our wanton shore?

Fantastic apparitions dance
drinking our smiles
like sky diamonds
winking in amusement.

Footprints follow us home
sandboxing our play
like these lonely words
lost fragile memories.

Haunting Farewells

I drifted with sunless cold
like breath on snowbound streets
lined by frozen smiles and
charcoal-burning eyes.

They guard my footprints
leading back to you
your final words
farewell's chilling part.

We remember our alone
always lost in love
your cry goodbye
haunting me tonight.

Lost Fables

A lyrical empath saw me
writing of lost times and loves
she rewrote and taught me
I can't remember who I was.

I share my lost fables
sailing on wilder shores
onto your northern view
of fires we shared together.

Where has the years gone
our path across
look within your soul
like me it's still right here.

Candelabra' ing Delight

Laniakea lanterns our vast path
through time ancient and anew
candelabra' ing our delight
as children of the sun.

We venture across in wonder
capacious minds tinkering
every age finds marvels
till they lose their shine.

How will our sojourn complete
as time winds down our clock
brilliant light we share
a love we'll never leave.

Casting Smiles

Your glance rewrote me
each time you catch mine
surreptitiously shared
unmasking our delight.

Hands tangle in moments
taking charge of us
thoughts crash surprised
sharing clever smiles.

Holding us our eyes stay
like we've anchored offshore
decisions now cast
we reef our sails.

Breadcrumb Semaphores

Spacetime's sneaky metaphor
wraps around your gazing eyes
gets into deep thought
as transfixed you lose yourself.

Thinking you've been fooled
breadcrumb semaphores
unmask its joke as
smiles bring you back.

You make up new words
showing us where you've been
transfixed we realize
you've made us all up too.

Ubiquitous Shadows

We live these days
under a strange sun
writing about shadows
across its ubiquitous light.

Yet there are some here
who glitter among us
their stunning words
shine behind our eyes.

You share such light
holding our words dear
such articulate semantics
resonates within all of us.

Remembering Forget-Me-Nots

Lost in fleeting moments
as you gift a glance
my scrambled thoughts
fall out of time onto yours.

Forget-me-nots take me
seducing my mind
such delicious elixirs
who am I now I've forgotten.

Wandering we always knew
wild shores have kept us
closer now we remember
you always found me.

Ravishing Sophistication

Your storms lash surprise
assailing my eyes, mind
ravishing sophistication as
euphoric imagination reigns.

Toasting champagning lips
upon your crème brûlée
I savor everything sweet
collapsing our wave.

Thoughts wild scatter
on dawn's exhilarated kiss
abandoning night's crazy
we rave into tomorrow.

Mnemosyne

American School Shootings

Thurston High School.
Columbine High School.
Heritage High School.
Deming Middle School.
Fort Gibson Middle School.
Buell Elementary School.
Lake Worth Middle School.
University of Arkansas.
Junipero Serra High School.
Santana High School.
Bishop Neumann High School.
Pacific Lutheran University.
Granite Hills High School.
Lew Wallace High School.
Martin Luther King, Jr. High School.
Appalachian School of Law.
Washington High School.
Conception Abbey.
Benjamin Tasker Middle School.
University of Arizona.
Lincoln High School.
John McDonogh High School.
Red Lion Area Junior High School.
Case Western Reserve University.
Rocori High School.
Ballou High School.
Randallstown High School.
Bowen High School.
Red Lake Senior High School.
Harlan Community Academy High School.
Campbell County High School.
Milwee Middle School.
Roseburg High School.
Pine Middle School.
Essex Elementary School.
Duquesne University.
Platte Canyon High School.
Weston High School.
West Nickel Mines School.
Joplin Memorial Middle School.
Henry Foss High School.
Compton Centennial High School.
Virginia Tech.
Success Tech Academy.
Miami Carol City Senior High School.
Hamilton High School.
Louisiana Technical College.
Mitchell High School.
E.O. Green Junior High School.
Northern Illinois University.
Lakota Middle School.
Knoxville Central High School.
Willoughby South High School.
Henry Ford High School.
University of Central Arkansas.
Dillard High School.
Dunbar High School.
Hampton University.
Harvard College.
Larose-Cut Off Middle School.
International Studies Academy.
Skyline College.
Discovery Middle School.
University of Alabama.
DeKalb School.
Deer Creek Middle School.
Ohio State University.
Mumford High School.
University of Texas.
Kelly Elementary School.
Marinette High School.
Aurora Central High School.
Millard South High School.
Martinsville West Middle School.
Worthing High School.
Millard South High School.
Highlands Intermediate School.
Cape Fear High School.
Chardon High School.
Episcopal School of Jacksonville.
Oikos University.
Hamilton High School.
Perry Hall School.
Normal Community High School.
University of South Alabama.
Banner Academy South.
University of Southern California.
Sandy Hook Elementary School.
Apostolic Revival Center Christian School.
Taft Union High School.
Osborn High School.
Stevens Institute of Business and Arts.
Hazard Community and Technical College.
Chicago State University.
Lone Star College-North.
Cesar Chavez High School.
Price Middle School.
University of Central Florida.
New River Community College.
Grambling State University.
Massachusetts Institute of Technology.
Ossie Ware Mitchell Middle School.
Ronald E. McNair Discovery Academy.
North Panola High School.
Carver High School.
Agape Christian Academy.
Sparks Middle School.
North Carolina A&T State University.
Stephenson High School.
Brashear High School.
West Orange High School.
Arapahoe High School.
Edison High School.
Liberty Technology Magnet High School.
Hillhouse High School.
Berrendo Middle School.
Purdue University.
South Carolina State University.
Los Angeles Valley College.
Charles F. Brush High School.
University of Southern California.
Georgia Regents University.
Academy of Knowledge Preschool.
Benjamin Banneker High School.
D. H. Conley High School.
East English Village Preparatory Academy.
Paine College.
Georgia Gwinnett College.
John F. Kennedy High School.
Seattle Pacific University.
Reynolds High School.
Indiana State University.
Albemarle High School.
Fern Creek Traditional High School.
Langston Hughes High School.
Marysville Pilchuck High School.
Florida State University.
Miami Carol City High School.
Rogers State University.
Rosemary Anderson High School.
Wisconsin Lutheran High School.
Frederick High School.
Tenaya Middle School.
Bethune-Cookman University.
Pershing Elementary School.
Wayne Community College.
J.B. Martin Middle School.
Southwestern Classical Academy.
Savannah State University.
Harrisburg High School.
Umpqua Community College.
Northern Arizona University.
Texas Southern University.
Tennessee State University.
Winston-Salem State University.
Mojave High School.
Lawrence Central High School.
Franklin High School.
Muskegon Heights High School.
Independence High School.
Madison High School.
Antigo High School.
University of California-Los Angeles.
Jeremiah Burke High School.
Alpine High School.
Townville Elementary School.
Vigor High School.
Linden McKinley STEM Academy.
June Jordan High School for Equity.
Union Middle School.
Mueller Park Junior High School.
West Liberty-Salem High School.
University of Washington.
King City High School.
North Park Elementary School.
North Lake College.
Freeman High School.
Mattoon High School.
Rancho Tehama Elementary School.
Aztec High School.
Wake Forest University.
Italy High School.
NET Charter High School.
Marshall County High School.
Sal Castro Middle School.
Marjory Stoneman Douglas High School.
Great Mills High School.
Central Michigan University.
Huffman High School.
Frederick Douglass High School.
Forest High School.
Highland High School.
Dixon High School.
Santa Fe High School.
Noblesville West Middle School.
University of North Carolina Charlotte.
STEM School Highlands Ranch.
Edgewood High School.
Palm Beach Central High School.
Providence Career & Technical Academy.
Fairley High School (school bus).
Canyon Springs High School.
Dennis Intermediate School.
Florida International University.
Central Elementary School.
Cascade Middle School.
Davidson High School.
Prairie View A&M University.
Atascocita High School.
Central Academy of Excellence.
Cleveland High School.
Robert E. Lee High School.
Cheyenne South High School.
Grambling State University.
Blountville Elementary School.
Holmes County, Mississippi (bus).
Prescott High School.
College of the Mainland.
Wynbrooke Elementary School.
UNC Charlotte.
Riverview Florida (school bus).
Second Chance High School.
Carman-Ainsworth High School.
Willwáw Elementary School.
Monroe Clark Middle School.
Central Catholic High School.
Jeannette High School.
Eastern Hills High School.
De Anza High School.
Ridgway High School.
Reginald F. Lewis High School.
Saugus High School.
Pleasantville High School.
Waukesha South High School.
Oshkosh High School.
Catholic Academy of New Haven.
Bellaire High School.
North Crowley High School.
McAuliffe Elementary School.
South Oak Cliff High School.
Texas A&M University-Commerce.
Sonora High School.
Western Illinois University.
Oxford High School.
Robb Elementary School.
Goddard Junior High.

Newtown

Ghosts live in Newtown
frozen in Summer
ceremonial priests chant
a haunting unlike any other.

Streets devour footprints
they all disappear
clouds race away like yachts
there's no finish line.

Churches cry for prayers
despair paints skies
there's no music here
even thought is gone.

American Eulogy

We cook in melancholic stew
enlightened by political salt
terrified as united states fall
embarrassed by a reborn traitor.

Our children wait for justice
elementary children sacrificed
black brothers & sisters murdered
Liberty raped by republican greed.

Are you watching and waiting
our climate a Venusian firestorm
as water tears from the dead
cremating the American Dream.

Crying Trees

Mommy, where's daddy?
Brutal floods my heart
I'm blind to everything
nowhere left to go.

Violence mobs my mind
they dragged him away
such hatred in those eyes
he was loved by everyone.

Trees crying all around
their arms weary of us
he built their homes
Baby, he's in heaven now.

Shackled & Tormented

Our roads were paved by
brothers and sisters
chained in blindness
beaten over pretense.

How did we lose our way
lost empires dust history
ignorance paid their fee
ours looms just ahead.

Minds shackled and tormented
bodies hung in trees
how many lives do we kill
before we crush our souls?

Burning Ice

Wake up chills prey on me
More souls gone
Cops abandoned us
When recourse demands
Did you step up to burn their ice?
Does anyone white see?
Living a nothinged life
Another son lays before me
Another mother shrieking on her knees.
Why does reason stop and killing acquit?
Courts embracing murder.
Is this your true or are you real?
What will it take for you?
Your child too?

Raped

No longer alone suddenly terrified
aghast eyes demand escape
hands boxing like I was taught
voice screaming into darkness.

Pain finds all of me grounded
my clothes ripped away
he thrusts me harder down
bleeding my eyes refuse to see.

I am alone being raped again
he knew where I lived
America keeps looking away
because I love myself.

Enthralling Poetic Dance

Melancholic eyes look out
as I remember
stories we shared.

Our worlds collide as the
song is familiar and the
dance still enthralls.

Yours is a treasure
delightfully told;
mine is the mirror of our dance.

We look to decide on our next word,
yet knowing it's always
been the same.

Shattered Passion

Maybe you never knew me
this time around
turbulent waves took us
our wildness washed ashore.

Empathic eyes sear mine
tormented hearts ablaze
we sine wave each day
ecstasy and agony.

Maybe we are still lost
an interlude of loneliness
even our passion shattered
won't stop us next time.

Your Chef D'ouvre

Your chef d'ouvre heartbreak
crazy eyes light our way
I know you want mine
reaching into your soul.

Black riders on my street
luring me to yours
our lost time skies
confused moments rule.

Your magister ludi took me
bodhisattva'ing my game
no one plays like you
as we start again.

Tossing Poetic Shade

Silently our eyes hold on
sunlight writes how we feel
tossing poetic shade
as if we've been here before.

Clouds hurry to catch up
laughing in their rain
they kiss us goodbye
hot sands beg for more.

Time plays our song
even stars begin to dance
when Luna smiles
our poem is complete.

Forgotten Time

You took to me when
my hands misunderstood
and you laughed at my
simple pleasure of you.

Drowning at your touch
and unable to find words
you'd desire, I fell away
but you kept me then.

Yet time forgot us
as my look back still smiles
those wide eyes we had
when simple was everything.

Wampanoag's Trail

People of first light
we know your truth
deep mourning seeps
twelve thousand years massacred.

Children of our sun we are
only moments to share
destinies we've yet to see
as ancestors lie in wait.

Wampanoag's Trail leads us
amid Plymouth's trees
sacred steps still resonate
crying for your peace.

Baked Laughter

You knew who I would be
searing under your sky
even now as we cool
memories slice me apart.

Roaring music made our bed
you stole my eyes
a river we can't flee
riding our light home.

Shadows love to paint us
skipping stones in our waves
like baked laughter
pulling us back together.

Lonely Skies

You're just a dream
I could never reach
so I sing you my days
will you find me instead?

I write these songs so
in my night you'll find me
and when my wings fail,
you'll carry me with yours.

Yet dreams I find upon
my skies leave me hoping
that you're real and someday
you'll dream of me.

Haunting Apparitions

See your fury torching us
lost light surrounds me
moments confused scatter
as if time knew better.

I hold your last glance
simmering like a mirage
it rages throughout me
branding what's left.

Forsaken eyes can't escape
apparitions haunt us
shadows of what we were
when time returned.

Eyes of Ukraine

While we stand with yours
You can share these heartfelt lines
Haunted by today
We shoulder Ukraine's terror
How can we not feel their eyes.

Rapt Skies

Skies rapt look delights
Holding today for your spell
Will it rain or shine
Meet me on the road to find
Words that play our song again.

Who We Were

So alone you cannot think
wanting your footsteps
careening through me
while we're not ok.

Even moments we've lost
remembering our eyes
frantically playing us
while we laughed crazy.

Writing who we've become
words fell in love with us
a dance only we made
remembering who we were.

Wings

The caterpillar dreamt
awakening your butterfly
she let her mindset go
remember how you felt?

Years have become us
a dance we've enjoyed
no one made me like you
such is your song.

Skies reach for our embrace
new wings unfurling
shall we touch the sky
as we play in our forever?

Vibes

Reticent vibe sandstorms
littering cosmic debris
eyes free water
flooding our everything.

Conscious desire debates
showering us with now
broken hearts gasp for air
hot sand fills what's left.

You're a wave in my mind
shoring what we both want
when night dreams of us
remember our vibe.

Lyrical Souls

I met a poet tonight
her words played within us
songs no one else knew
she touched everything.

I met a human being
she shared her soul
days we'll never leave
laughing like no one.

I met you again my sweet
such is your searing mind
what does love mean
when everything is yours?

Stopping Time

Torn pages butterfly away
to bask in darkened words
masquerading like poetry
written as time stopped.

Whoever you have become
desert skies hold me
such vast emptiness
pours into what remains.

Your songs cloak me
cascading our lyrical rapport
rewriting who I am
till our time returns.

Silhouettes

Silhouettes masquerade as you
under my desert skies
our painter pauses
shadowing what's light.

Forms encourage us to tempt
bridging what we were
a song in your mind
ephemeral memories.

Stars between our eyes
shores we've yet to beach
as your brush makes me
taste my light in yours.

Mirages

Desert night sky rains stars
we're swept up in their light
mirages spellbind now
the sojourn of our lives.

Idyllic solitude chants
our thoughts are all alone
when you leave
promise tomorrow still sings?

Serendipity plays our hearts
ghosting who we were
as our sun dawns all others
will yours light upon mine?

Alkahests

Words tempt us to be
won't you stay
they love to slip into yours
opening up our lives.

Such is their design
masquerading as light
we give them wings
alkahests to open minds.

I story them together
painting days like an old friend
will you share yours
help us find who we want to be?

Dépaysement

One can still touch your stars
when darkness comes
dépaysement astonishes
like startled fallen leaves.

Senses clamor for one look
a song we sang
warmth of your eyes
fingers lingering on me.

One can still remember
chills making our music
even as sadness commands
who I was with you.

Words Become Us

Do you walk alone
writing beautiful words
just to keep you company
as they hold onto who we were.

Moonlit shadows follow them
taking all of you home
pieces that remind us
we're both a story in play.

We love to dance here
lost in yesterday
writing of us
healing who we've become.

Black Lives Matter

Our tears will not stop
for centuries
children have grown up scared
black lives matter.

America has been asleep
since the 17th century
do you love your children
they are our future.

Awash in systemic disease
our country is threatened
children are watching us
black lives matter.

Truth

America killed John Lennon
like King and Kennedy
your brothers and sisters
hanging from our trees.

How does reason flee
facing such monsters
It even said it's like us
pleading for your vote.

Our children follow us
their music our poetry
how will they remember
songs used against us.

Smiling Freckles

West coast jazz bops
sunborn freckles smile
making out on rooftops
we lived in another world.

Louis Armstronging tonight
like we never left
sailing out of Newport
queen gambiting today.

Desert skies ocean me now
writing about our deepness
such was your allure
sandstorming our now.

Baked Atmosphere

Atmospheres bake us
Falling starlight lifts our hearts
When your eyes alight
Mine dance like our first time here
Sailing our ocean of night

Wounded Spirits

Empty pages beg forgiveness
enlightening tomorrow
scanning eyes tempt
reading who we are.

Words conjure who we were
spellbinding our looks
would you quiet mine
like a sky that holds us?

Wounded spirits sear us
I touched you before
our vibe never let go
dancing like we knew it.

Racing Thoughts

Stunned chills meet your happy
they samba all over me
a silhouette of racing thoughts
walking my demure away.

Empty eyes flee us
apprehension loses its way
sunlight crashes our party
gathering what we've found.

Laughter rewrites our sighs
replenishing the empty night
even as day's light ebbs
I want to be your shore.

Samba Eyes

Breathless moments unwrap
words forget how to say
sighs moan for them
holding us hostage.

Turning time's eloquence
a reach we dare not stop
samba eyes locked
anticipation meets our lips.

Electric fingers race to touch
tasting our aphrodisiacal
exploding minds delight
letting us go again.

Desert Shores

Could we still watch us
unwrap time's paradox
both young and older
skating between what's real?

Your beautiful wings
nights we ventured
change who I've become
will any sky hold us?

We owned them all
walking on desert shores
fires and little loves running
we were never so bright.

Comfortable Storm

Emotional turbulence
ebbs across our deep
waves crash my now
holding our real captive.

One step closer to yours
my breath loses me
broken laughter seeks us out
paving what could be.

All alone we sing ourselves
casting looks like flowers
alluring to who we were
a comfortable storm

Fluorescent Gazes

Gathered in your light
featured in darling days
cunning shadows flee
like smiles spilling out.

Silhouettes mask a gasp
rainbows in your music
wings we've emboldened
mesmerizing everyone.

Fluorescent gazes beckon
like nights we wrote of us
across the searing sky
hands across our shores.

Sanguine Melancholia

Gray skies on desert minds
labyrinthian thoughts
I write them down
yet your memories escape.

It takes us apart now
waning a little at a time
such eloquent glances
my only recourse back.

Kind sanguine emotions
melancholia befriended us
sweet poignant hunger
beckons tomorrow's rain.

Emotional Debris

Only when our words fly
do we collaborate
a shared space between
our emotional debris.

Would you secret mine
taste what you desire
could you stay here too
change who we might be?

I remember meeting you
rushing energy as we loved it
making us up again
like we've been here before.

So Many Roads

Drumz circle held our beat
your solo meandering
mine looked for you
charming us at Stanford's Frost.

California under our feet
we had no idea
playing so many roads
one hundred shows.

Who were you I've wondered
ecstasy on our minds
blue light ruled
we forgot about the time.

Drums circle our beat
measuring delicious tempo
we khruangbin deeper
only brave dare with us.

Dancing waves envelop
they exotic our immersion
subtle chords bind
forgetting who we were.

Dripping wet we moment
our euphoria witnessed
an unbroken chain sung
euphoric and astonished.

Hookalaylee's Kiss

Sailing off Newport
Hookalaylee'ing her north coast
rushing alive on waves
to Camden's stone-cobbled.

Jazz on her summer day
backgammoned us
as we bantered sweet position
a coyness beside ourselves.

Sun kisses setting Moon
delightedly we followed
their twilight goodbye
our sweet hellos.

Twitterville

Twitter is like ice cream
a frozen imaginary moment
capturing all our hopes
as it fades over time.

We freeze them overnight
hoping they're real
even dreams are all in
alone in the night.

Dawn stings us awake
your voice just a memory
of our sweet time shared
we can't resist returning.

Melting Melancholic

You know our songs
melting our melancholic
imaging words we keep
even as they strike deep.

Delta time cannot see us
wanting you wrapped inside
I believed in your light
even as darkness took me.

I already have let you go
bound in our rain
like my desert sand now
releasing who we once were.

Poetic Memory

Rewriting poetic memory
words falter hurrying past
I feel them crashing
my eyes burn for yours.

So you'd smile at me
days we'd invent ourselves
making up new words
we knew we'd happen.

Desert snow begs for us
footprinting all alone
our moments cast in ice
reading who we've become.

Lost Dreams

I knew great sadness
she held me as a child
made me watch her pain
I felt every savage cast.

Walking in the woods
we cut down our terrible
in shock trees wept for us
giving up their arms.

They burned our souls
even scars remember
she cried for us in the night
our dreams never found us.

Chenzeme

Chenzeme debris reigns
another creature of light
fear holds our breath
we are no longer alone.

Unknown shadows guide us
a strange sun confuses
your body melds mine
we dare not venture alone.

Time has deserted us
leaving only despair
she races in our blood
stripping us of thought.

Petrichor

Enchanting Vibe

Your alluring vibe mesmerizes
enchanting petrichor
we slip underwater
envious sun tries to hold you.

Clear blue water envelopes
delicious vapor scents
you after sun and rain
imprisoned we fall in.

Moon steals all hearts
light flees in shadows
as you start to sing again
even the stars come out.

Time's Rainbow

No one knew like you
finding shadows in music
always saving my light
even when you were gone.

Finding your beautiful
songs still write me
a haunting muse
recalls our storms home.

Summer breaks within us
our time like rainbows
beautiful light in this rain
your song still plays me.

Your Electric Mind

Taken along inside your words
I ride hope's wildness
like horses running free
your electric mind rides me.

Roaming yours smiles persist
does anyone know you better
we share an aftertaste as
reading mine you laugh.

Alas, our crazy forty-fives
still resonate within us
whispering what we knew
wanting what we dream.

Uncertainty's Fate

You ask my eyes if I'm real
my uncertainty touch
measures your fate
as you decide mine.

We walk thoughts home
along our haunted roads
reaching for days unseen
as they crowd around us.

Comfortable darkness
lends its stealthy feel
tomorrow's glances beckon
sleeping with our dreams.

Walk with Me

I walked with you alone
not thinking straight
wondering why you're so
beyond anything I've met.

Before you stopped to
touch my soul and make me
didn't you know why
I'd still want you now?

I walk without you now
my desperate thoughts
looking for parts of me
you've taken with you.

Goodbye Look

Your eyes told me more
than I thought you might
say to me instead,
so we talked after all.

We danced around,
our words, our music
your eyes leading me,
mine thinking ahead.

But the song ended
and you took those
gentle eyes away,
leaving mine to say goodbye.

Jade Vase

Goodbye sweet tears of us
graced me with a kindness
such was my life in you
how much we loved us.

My days hold you inside
memory paints you back
rooms throughout my mind
I never knew you like I do now.

Goodbye my sweet
our joy a vessel we made
like a jade vase of smiles
I saved for yours.

Charade Me

You knew it was too late
words I've written to you
like yours who dance
making me want another.

Sauntered into such moments
searing delicious
laughing we remember
you found me first.

Charades domino your mind
writing about being taken
like how I want you
binding your lips on mine.

Haunted Glances

Remember that glance you
found on that sunstruck day
when I lost myself
back in time beside you?

You shared it as we laughed
finding ourselves
together
in its warm embrace.

We let it go one day,
yet still felt it around us,
as it slowly faded like a song;
its haunting memory devouring me.

Petrichor Ghosts

Silence embraces us
only our songs remain
like petrichor after rain
I'm left with your ghost.

Such is a foolish heart
we never shared sunlight
always a step away
a poem we never read.

Paradise lost still torments
even time lost count
Calliope warned me of you
a song without meaning.

Gardens On the Moon

If my wings find you alone
will you fly with me
soar against our crazy
sing your song in mine?

Led zeppelin our skies
planting gardens on the moon
teach me your laugh
let your hair down on me?

When your wings tire
can I carry you in mine
soar across our vast
make your thoughts sing?

Sun Rain

We are sun rain here
children under her love
taking our sweet light
your kiss finding mine.

She knows we're young
strong tempests delightful
deciphering her light
etched across our eyes.

We hurricane our own
they don't know us
will you remember me
laugh with me in our rain?

Kissing Sadie Hawkins

Your wings found me
such a beautiful mind
we've known all our lives
writing our lost stories.

I've walked you home
remembering our first dance
Sadie Hawkins kissed me
you knew me before I did.

See how we hurricane
you storm my shores
songs we sing still fly
as my words find yours.

Desire's Memes

Such a look your eyes take
maddening in their disguise
we gambit from afar
sipping some of your light.

It rushes painting us real
like a beautiful viral meme
captures imaginations into
my stunned addiction.

If time's illusion holds you
sweet memories sink inside
like a river we stream upon
mapping our desires.

Trading Glimpses

We both know what happened
your writing electric
mine holding your eyes
days we've made for us.

Eyes trading glimpses
won't you share your smile
these days evaporating
like tastes we used to share.

You know my map now
do you want me here
our crazy laughter
remembers who we were.

Finding Your Vibe

If time is just a picture frame
holding all your sweet smiles
all my walls photograph them
shaping time for both of us.

Painting my mind around us
so I can dance to your vibe
Montana still beckons
shall we fly tonight?

We'll build new memories
whispering who we were
you handstand a question
knowing all about my answer.

Making Us Up

So we say we're real
then it's something beautiful
even when lost in our rain
I know who you are.

Sometimes we talk for hours
whispering of love
coming to see you
rainbow eyes laughing.

It's why we play together
making us up as we go
your fire still storms
you know who I am.

Tripping Our Electric

You knew my smile yours
tripping our electric
we captured everything
unable to let go of us.

Won't you take my hand
stoke our fire tonight
when time wakes us
will my kiss make yours?

Gonna wait till you laugh
baby you own my words
why else do we play here
dreams we know are ours.

Like No Other

Grateful vibe overwhelms
every song we shared
pieces of us crazy love
strewn across our eyes.

Sometimes walking all alone
I find your voice
hidden in beautiful light
a taste like no other.

Scarlet flower mirrors you
gorgeous wings beheld
teaching me who I am
a love like no other.

Dappled Time

Wearing light like a poem
you hold on to my eyes
reading dappled time
we rewrite who we were.

Days tumble out of control
trying on each other
their debris surrounds us
settling on evening's dusk.

Daises sprout smiles you own
our laughter glitters
like words we made up
cherishing tomorrow's.

Dragons

You knew as I laughed
owning words I'm writing
your flames consumed me
as my dragon flew.

When will we stop our crazy
beyond forever moments
does time capture us
what we've already felt.

Did you find me wanting
photographs of your smile
I've been here before
you said I was yours.

Like Rain

We all share time together
dipping our toes here
wanting your hand
dreams I have tonight.

Falling in love like rain on you
kissing yesterday goodbye
you paint me like no one
unwrapping our today.

So nightfall takes us
wondering if you want me
my words lost at sea
dreaming of yours.

Falling Down the Rabbit Hole

Gonna find out who I am
you're a beautiful poem
the light you share
even my dark flees.

Days wordy rappinghood'ing
delightful ways we touch
stories make us real
falling down our rabbit hole.

All the colors in your mind
painting mine
they tell me who you are
lighting my road to you.

Your Way

Now I realize your ways
a tide eroding words
love our strongest poison
smoking both of us.

We've said goodbye before
our shadows never met
eyes on forever shores
a kiss lost for waiting.

And words we forgave
wondering why I stayed
even our laughter cried
no one ever set us free.

Killing Smiles

How does anyone stay
our minds open everywhere
walking alone reading you
laughing between words.

How do we decide us
wondering if we're real
I'm nowhere waiting
even your smile kills.

How do I know I'm real
your mind still commands
I was yours before I knew
you were the only one.

Our Vibe

Your vibe moves shadows
even sunlight dances
will you hold my hand
twirl your laughter for me?

If I write about your deep
will you let me dive in
explore who we might be
a look you've already sold.

We found our lost days
safeguarding us
a song inside a dream
playing our vibe now.

Hidden Smiles

Chills find your friendship
masking yesterdays
your gorgeous mind
captures everyone.

We're all playing similars
clones of hidden smiles
they rapt us in darkness
hugging what we need.

Promise you will remember
tasting my stolen look
your picture burned in me
how could we we forget?

Glistening Gazes

Dreaming of another sun
her light a midnight seduction
touches my dark wings
as they warm yours.

Aah my choice takes us
these days now lost
she knows who I am
falling into her gaze.

So I paint her back here
glistening on my brush
her smile a long-lost fret
as she warms to mine.

Bare Trees

Silence when we're gone
eyes riding rogue waves
summer ran away today
loving our bare trees.

I'll miss sunstruck looks
you painted everyone's
even mine lost
stepping in another memory.

Goodbye desert skies
sewing together our light
they find us alone now
feeding on strange nights.

Light's Truth

Darkness covets light's truth
your moves embrace mine
shadows paint lost words
dancing like we want to.

Our breath takes hold
forgetting who needs it
even laughter runs free
peeking at our eyes.

You already knew my name
yours branding me
looking for a lover
we story them together.

Gardens

So we come down to us
if you want to make me
I've shown you my universe
does yours forever too?

Gardens planted play us
their lap up our light
wanting to see if we care
do you find them real?

You're somewhere here
making songs about us
they still sing to me
enveloping uncertainty.

Musing California

Thank you as we depart
astonishing electric vibe
days loved every second
even when they left us.

We became new songs
burning till we let go
all our words magic
conjuring us up again.

Sweet California made love
musing for both of us
I lost myself yesterday
when I found you here.

Flowers for Yesterday

You've been haunting me
like flowers crying in the rain
they hold my eyes
tearing for yesterday.

I inked your goodbye card
our favorite song colors
just to tell you someday
what I couldn't say today.

Champagne we never tasted
just our hopeful glitteratti
rainbows sprinkled in our eyes
as our song finally ended.

My Muse

Cold breath gets inside
unraveling our pasts
wondering were we real
will the temptress wake.

Surreptitious lips own time
conspiring against ours
her forever look
a smile only she can handle.

Stories we've left behind
sweet muse of my words
I fell in love with you
bending time for us.

Holding Yesterday's Light

Streets washing cold wind
we've forgotten our way
I am the poem that remembers
holding yesterday's light.

As everything is lost
even my words flee
maybe they'll understand
if you ever taste them.

I was always just a mirror
your songs found me
as cold wind's wings fly
where will we go now?

Unwritten Poems

Rain loves to find us alone
she's more than we know
washing what's true
leaving our naked light.

If you touch me like her
would you mirror me
wake me to have you
piano my sad smile?

We are just unwritten poems
trying to find us
you gifted me my words
they fell in love with yours.

Strange Evenings

When poets escape
the scene we're wanting
will the words left waiting
still ask for love?

It's a strange evening
cold winds on our shores
will you save my soul
let my light find yours?

So we make us up again
editing who we were
poems we never wrote
wondering if you're real.

Lost Poems

Words know I'm vulnerable
they work to set me free
yours rewrote what I sing
will we ever reread us?

If I make you feel again
will you want me here
alkahest my dreams
make me want yours?

Lost poems clutter my mind
reminding me of lovers
all our crazy laughing
your words made mine.

Never Meeting Ourselves

I've known you forever
but we've never met.
You picked me up when
I awoke and you
stayed with me when
I was dying.
A touch from your
shared smile sparked life
when everyone else
turned away.
And the light around you
shines inside me when others
brought only darkness.

Lost Sighs

Sighing winds hug mine
they know you
as my band plays on
can't find a way home.

Friday nights we were all in
sipping words with Insignia
laughing on slippery slopes
no shore held our wave.

And now these lonely words
flee from my storm
your lyrical lighthouse
singing of our lost love.

Burning Together

What will your tomorrow eyes
find under cover today
will they scream my name
laughing as we stitch time.

You found me first baby
stealing my glance
your songs playing me
no idea they'd burn us.

Wove your light into rainbows
wrapping up my words
in songs we played
till our madness fades.

Sunlight in the Rain

Nothingness surrounds us
yet you made us real
days fell for us like love
we had nowhere else to go.

I feel you in my rain
sunlight plays your taste
stars blanket dreams
my wings still find you.

Yet morning chills
smiles we shared
your eyes a poem I write
will you ever see mine?

Fading Sighs Like Stars at Dawn

First stars sprinkled across
sky's vast canvas
your distant eyes gazing
upon me as I look for yours.

In these thoughts and visions
of mine, of yours
eidolons within me sing
sharing your songs.

So as the sky hides us
and your dream of me fades
by early dawn
I sigh dreaming of you.

Your Secret Key

Color me you today
as we roam together
painting ourselves
who we will become tonight.

Your familiar grace
touching what's beautiful
as I've come to trade myself
for today's rain around you.

May I have your secret key
held within you for just tonight
will you grant me one wish
so I can hear you laughing?

Of Loves Lost & Found

Your gorgeous desolation
thrills me
as I gaze at you
sharing our stage in the stars.

Your dappled light
beside dusky evening trees
mesmerizes love found in
your gorgeous alluring eyes.

Your sad ephemeral smile
touches me deeply
as we remember other tales
of loves lost and found.

Tasting Today

Dancing, the night awaits
for your morning as
I look inside this empty space
your mindful place here without me
and I sing your poetic name
while your joyous laughter
finds us both
embracing
our sweet taste of today
how I long to hear my name
upon your lips
when you remember me.

September

September knew you had me
you fell in love with her
when we stopped pretending
even our laughter knew better.

Breathing your amazing smile
I forget who I wanted to be
your pictures all over mine
who will we become now?

We somewhere our intentions
wondering is love enough?
I don't want to be alone
you're everywhere I go.

Exquisite Eyes

Your moment became mine
falling in love
can you touch my sound
make me hear yours?

So we take flight again
soaring over gorgeous
fields of our beautiful
reminding who we are.

Lost in time you found me
unfolding a universe of light
spending my days chasing
your exquisite eyes.

Shadows in Color

Don't you want me coloring
songs in your eyes
even if we're sad now
you know I'll hold you tight.

I've seen you in the dark
won't you dive deeper
mesmerize my light
wrap me inside yours?

Laughing we run on shadows
between astonished looks
gifting everyone we meet
colors of our imagination.

Lingering Scent

Petrichor scent lingers on me
a sweet kiss you were here
as rain's envy tries me on
scattering my thoughts.

Hollow coves remind me
we've shared our storms
tasting salt in the air
sand between our toes.

We violined our days together
weathering a sensual tapestry
rapt by your gorgeous crazy
I'm left alone in the rain.

Unread Poetry

We were just unread poems
words remembering us
our candle burned hot
as yesterday's light forgets.

I used to read your eyes
like paintings in the sky
they loved how we spoke
days charading as us.

You knew me before I did
songs to make me
beautiful incantations
living inside me now.

Homeless Words

Writing songs of you
my words seem lost
searching for who we are
as our worlds collide.

Your hands throw kisses
scattered colors reign
as we paint our lives over
days we lost ourselves.

I saved your smiles inside
they hold me together
wondering who I am
my words still homeless.

Staying in Your Moment

There are people in our lives
Love shares their souls
looking to our happy
they've gifted theirs.

My muse electrifies thought
writing who I have become
I adore her earth spirit
stepping in her garden.

We soar night skies
they blanket love
driving us crazy
staying in every moment.

Baking Us

Such was our pas de deux
a dance of two in one
spent like puddled rain
we even kissed our shadows.

Dusk's surreptitious embrace
lover's youth found within
yearning to find lips
enrapturing our words.

Falling into met eyes
words writing within us
passion takes our heat
baking who we've become.

Strange Shores

Castoff onto strange shores
I came of age for you
holding your light
shadows of a dream.

Shipwrecked, lost, and alone
days have forgotten time
as moments unbind us
my thoughts sing of you.

Moonlight footprints me
wandering like I'm crazy
into our new world
waiting till you dream of me.

Lost Rain

I'd known that look you wore
taking me outside forever
when you were gone
no one was left inside.

Imagining your worlds
these days our crazy
we campfire at home now
will anyone remember us?

You saw me one night
writing these words to you
all our goodbyes
scripted like lost rain.

Sharing Light & Rain

Ocean and Cloud shared Rain
washing our eyes
they tugged at our hearts
remembering yesterday.

Sun and Moon shared Light
drenching our spirit
they dried our eyes
thinking of today.

Dusk and Evening kissed
holding us spellbound
they cherished our minds
dreaming of tomorrow.

Transcendence

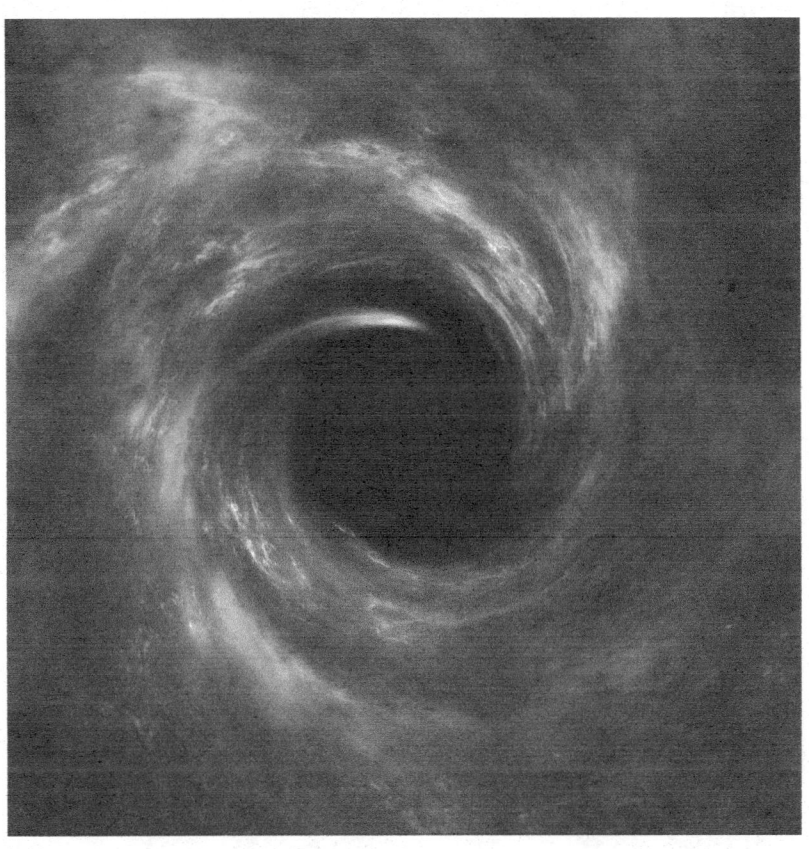

Transcendence

You know it was our time
when the rain took you
we fell apart that day
unable to save ourselves.

You left us all in tears
where were we when
you cried for help
why was I alone apart?

We need your heart here
our minds desert lands now
will you take our hands
to light our eyes again?

Alone you decembered us
turning minds to ice
we lost everything
sanity fled without you.

You've healed us since
together making songs
through our dark clouds
raining your beautiful.

We never lost your heart
desert minds flourish
as holding hands now
we found the light our eyes lost.

Bound in Time

Wraiths sing of distant time
of energies within us
of clarity we once knew
before stars and galaxies.

Awakened by uncertainty
dawn moments remake us
creatures of simultaneous change
we bridge all worlds.

Transcendence reimagined
is it a wonder we remain
teachers of ancient lore
we bind our love to yours.

By Your Side

Would you hold my hand
steeling our minds tonight
eyes still lost alone
following what we dreamt.

Secret potions trade hellos
mixing our delicious
desert winds strip us
taking what's left.

Together everyone gathers
who we all might be
ebbing time's shores
onto our wilder moments.

Sand Bridges

Light like you in my eyes
touches us
searing as my desert sand
teaching who we've become.

Scattered emotional debris
changes our real
tears bind who we were
souls adrift waiting.

Building bridges on smiles
we paint days like promises
incandescent captivated moments
freeing what's real.

Abandoned Masquerade

Thoughts run inside you
dropping time's masquerade
charades played us both
breaking all the rules.

Meeting in wildfires
we even whispered hello
love always held
making everything real.

Winter broke summer's spell
forsaking us
as spring loves autumn's dust
it'll miss our laughter.

Writing Us Here

Writing songs to find us
playing them to relax
winging it after dark
just to make laughter work us.

Does your vibe make mine
easing into futures
everything follows
a dance without end.

Imagining you're here now
talking like lost poets
sharing tears to remember
who we might have been.

Lyrical Dreams

Goodbye dreaming shores
you surfed me all along
such is your waking light
even dawn fell in love.

Remember searing fires
our lyrical invented us
igniting what we said
sharing what we became.

Be happy in your world
our words made us up
if you find me someday
tell me you were real.

Desert's Wings

When I think of you now
everything evaporates
living in a desert mirage
we were our only song.

Being us we sang crazy
writing of lovers lost
sand in our pockets
like stars in our eyes.

We'll miss what we meant
only whispers knew us
find your wings baby
soar like you own it.

Treasured Canopies

And into us days met
holding onto what matters
playing like children
a hope we'll canopy.

Only when you look inside
will you find my moment
painting lyrical memes
a song in your name.

Love like a child's wonder
treasures we'll never lose
take my hand, sweet
a dance we'll forever.

Sighs

Awakened we move in light
imagining today
who we might become
what we dare leave behind.

Our language mesmerizes
promises our lips gift
trying to wrap up yours
waiting till they unfold.

Staring after your laughter
I want to be your sigh
our shadowed emotion
crowding out our words.

Sautéd Ghosts

What will you take away
saying I need your space
playing with your words
my crazy holds yours as we fly.

Believable ghosts own us
even when we're lost
your touch remembers
dreams we've sautéd.

When our light asks for real
who do you dream of
after we know who we are
do you still want mine?

Measuring Magical

We tune in listening to you
measuring our magical
a song we've never heard
diving deep into yours.

Moments hold you here
like our favorite look
a glance that stole me
changing our words.

Affection tastes melancholic
a kiss we've shared
touching a kindness
you play me in your mind.

Blank Canvases

As you dreamt of us
I fell into your words
like a sandstorm's kiss
painting our adobe real.

Surreal gorgeous music
playing on your shore
should we dance tonight
make our sky love again.

Calling for your moment
we're lost writing alone
there's always another
empty canvas wanting us.

Crowded Ghosts

Why do you still stay
footprinting my soul
crazy fingers linger
as you write me here.

Something touches what's left
a dance we both invited
words making goodbyes
a sadness knifing through us.

Laughter still binds us
fleeing into secrets
did you ever keep mine
hugging crowded ghosts?

Our Deepness

Glimpses deepen us
Waves upon these crowded shores
A touch of core fire
Held in a river of light
Destined to become our real.

Your Reach

Your real touches us
Flowering across our vast
As these words streetlight
My thoughts become autumn's rain
A reach of my real to yours.

Sandcastling Time

Clouds rain sunbeam's hue
eyes glint like light on sand
sighing winds canopy
cobwebbing what remains.

Twilight settles like dust
holding on to yesterday
mesmerized portents
plead for our magic.

Captivated stillness sets
sandcastling time
under mirrored skies
we outrun our storms.

Clouds on Rain

I could write about you
even as we make us up
creatures of light
mirroring what's real.

Time decides who we are
roaming sandstorms alone
we photograph moments
wanting to be in yours.

You move into my space
like clouds on rain
would you still stay with me
as our story changes us?

Dreaming Apparitions

Would you wander my skies
soaring free
your wings against mine
eclipsing the moon?

When memory flees
will you read my poetry
capture who we once were
imagine our real again?

As sighs recall deep love
time once knew our fate
mirroring what we'd become
words our apparitions dreamt.

Time's Paradox

When we find time for us
do you hear my song
playing your moment
melodies only we hear.

Darkness begs us to leave
dancing warriors of light
laugh at our childs play
we wonder at theirs.

Time's paradox unfolds
choosing who we become
inside an ocean of light
you write my only poem.

Desert Vibe

Sails tempt desert wind
Coursing to find mirages
As we vibe tonight
Will you walk us to the shore
Make poetry reign like stars?

Our Moment

We share a moment
Eclipsing time's komorebi
Dancing with our light
As each step finds us today
Held by forever's present

Sparked Glimpses

Do you make me up
conjuring my real for yours
let our ghosts run free
like clouds crying rain.

Skies race beckoning
thoughts we both want
dissolving like memories
written in our eyes.

Stories find out we knew
when glimpses spark
imagining who we might be
trading looks like we did.

Lost Sunbeams

Sad, happy, I'm just in love
singing of your dark eyes
they hold me forever
showing me who I am.

Sunburnt clouds taste us
you're all over my surprise
spinning up our music
no one finds us today.

Sipping morning dew
your warm beside mine
lost sunbeams awaken
showing us who we are.

Luminescence

Ghosts sit beside us wanting
remembering how we feel
they wander everywhere
never realizing who they were.

Songs and light escape them
sighing like eventide's fade
empyreal enchantments
craving for your touch.

Tricking light's rapture
glimmers play our eyes
like elvish magicians
beckoning one more day.

Orchestrating Us

Moments forget who we were
as if time has secreted us
across illusionary footprints
written in what we want.

Stealthness holds our breath
wondering if we should
our parallel universes
shaping who we've become.

So we tune ourselves
orchestrating us now
our one last chance
playing our final hand.

Sea of Tranquility

We dreamt together
earthshine side of the moon
light and dark strangers
even dawn overslept.

Blacklight skies forever
eyes crater starlight
tranquility reimagined
as gravity stole away.

Oceans taunt memory
days we sandcastled love
regretting childhood's end
finally understanding us.

Eventide's Wake

Your lost touch weeps in me
like rain flooding my eyes
confused moments flee
stranding me in yesterday.

Your scent lingers here
intoxicating my mind
in everyone I see now
your spirit pleads to be.

Yet as eventide fades
these memories persist
dawning new dreams
of who I once was.

Wild Horses

Poignant liquid sun makes us
electric eyes open mine
walking together through
doors of lost memories.

Alluring us with scents
such times being alive
dancing like wild horses
independent souls on fire.

Days would play us over
painting our song
across skies of delight
making our night.

Cacophonies of Darkness

Obsession's depth grips
thought escapes
it holds me hostage
echos corridor my mind.

Passion's wings sky me
playing you over again
diving deep into possession
I flee upper days of darkness.

Cacophonies battle for light
courting skirmishes
drenched in love
eyes mirror our desire.

Gossamer Wings

Ethereal's present gifts now
bridging paradoxical moments
caught in quantum space
we're held on gossamer wings.

Thought becomes us
nourishing our child
writing us here
who we once were.

Frozen in time's river
transcendent designs
reality patiently awaits
who we'll actually become.

Melancholic Rain

Melancholic rain devours
surreptitious lips part
coldly ask goodbye
haunting our last look.

Disguised eyes escape
even thought crashes
dark secrets roam our sky
cryptically clouding us.

Caught in emotional waves
we drown in yesterday
grounded butterflies flee
consuming last hopes.

Echos of Us

Sadness comforts who we were
as thought cast shadows
only echos remain
days we sang as one.

Shared beams flowered
like sunstruck rainbows
they remind me of you
as fires recast who we are.

Time has a way of forgetting
as it embraces another
I knew we would leave
who we could have been.

Memories in Shadows & Light

Poetic eyes show me how
they hold onto mine
like past lives yearning
just to feel light again.

I'm dancing in language
words pry open my mind
memories beg for a hello
looking for traces of you.

Your vision mirrors me
like shadows and light
love touches our space
flooding my eyes.

Enchanting Tides of Light

Drifting thought evanescences
mesmerizing what remains
like our last sip of us
we'll savor through time.

Enchanting tides of light
recall who we were
caught in your gravity
they hold on to me.

Songs of yesterday flee
each time they play us
all I wanted to say
is written in my eyes.

Poetic Light

Your words ask me to dance
holding us as we fall
deeper into today's sky
like light waxing poetic.

Moving together in time
we're bound in thought
accelerating our days
just to play in another.

Desire never asks to go
she holds our eyes
a delightful encounter
laughing as we crash.

Melancholic Wine

Breathing your atmosphere
will we human today
embrace a piano'ed lullaby
dance together like shadows.

My skies weep now
dreaming of your clouds
they say we never rained
waiting for a secret shore.

Sharing melancholic wine
we found us
poetics our first kiss
she knew we'd want more.

Bene Gesserit Dance

Your empathic bene gesserit
wraps inside my thoughts
even time opens her gates
promising another dance.

Keys piano our song
voices command desire
desert heat seduces
stars beckon our play.

We've paved tomorrow's road
walking our way home
will you sing for me
as this dance begins?

Desert Rain

I knew you'd say goodbye
moments when we met
feeling our words
songs we've always sung.

We couldn't sing another's
they all slipped away
like rain in desert skies
or smiles kissing our eyes.

Ghosting dark years past
night wings say hello
our haunted dreams
songs no one else plays.

Measuring Our Fate

Muad'Dib's desert tears
even mice know
walking like ghosts
on ocean shores still dry.

Your touch finds us
alive against her wind
held in hourglassed prisons
time measures our fate.

Children's minds beckon
they pray for what we've lost
will you stay tonight
dream of them with me?

Ghosted Smiles

You found me enigmatic
our questions unanswered
my crazy apprehension
for your smile to stay.

We left the night cold
our wine untouched
as we knew not who we
really wanted us to become.

Where has our poetry gone
smiles ghosting us
my crazy despair haunts
our eyes have never met.

Remembering Us

In a space we left behind
confused moments linger
wrapped around our minds
leading us to who we are.

I knew you many times before
holding my breath
time laughed as we stopped
knowing where we'd go.

You stayed in my light
dancing your poetic
each song remade us
recalling who we were.

A Longer View

I remember you finding me
mirroring our deep jazz
being who we wanted
taking us back home.

In a way we already knew
sojourning in time
our slow dance never stops
a taste we love to cook.

Secreting a longer view
realms cycle as we learn
each one teaches us
till we find home again.

Lost Sailors

Since you've known my only
we've played together
sadness saves us
in our lost sailor crazy.

Beware of my distant songs
colors wrap inside you
they know us well
poetry our shadows cast.

All of these words sing
revealing tales shared
as we move into light
shores sand our beautiful.

Skipping Light Stones

Twilight's magic encases
you sunglass my eyes
chills crowd our minds
scattering reason's logic.

Drinking light like wine
I take yours inside
sipping on my shadow
you laugh at my darkness.

Music making love to us
you blink your smile
skipping stones to me
holding on as we submerge.

Forever Goodbyes

Sunrise holds you in my eyes
septembering memories
playing your guitar
as autumn wounds us.

Locked inside my mind
leftover words
a poem you'll never read
till you open me up again.

Your music still haunts
sharing what's in your head
forever goodbyes as
someone else is in your bed.

Comfortable Melancholy

Time sips melancholic comfortable
reigning for absent glints
windows left yearning
yesterday's real has fled.

Seems like you knew
seductive dark begged us
glistening allures
as you took mine

Careless fables used me
saying what I wanted
we loved to play them
editing out our fears.

Shadows On My Soul

Your emotions blanket my sky
like shadows on my soul
will you free yours
so you can find mine?

Roads begging for footprints
map our minds today
dreaming of them
you ask me to dance.

Skating around our words
wrapped under new skies
unable to free myself now
I wonder if you're real.

Emotional Turbulence

Dragon's fire licks astonishment
as your wave overwhelms
it claws like emotional turbulence
staggering onto my wilder shores.

Your ardent tide's flood pleads
will you stay in my crazy
embrace what you cannot see
swim in my mind's light.

We ocean our water together
chasing storms' delight
even as nightfall unmasks us
there's fire upon your deep.

Sandless Shores

Islands crisscross our skies
portals to find your smiles
daydreaming of shared light
on their sandless shores.

Clouds rush onto mine
kissing your laughter
memories of days to be
like living on the moon.

Mountains ask for patience
scaling my ocean of words
will you share your real
make footprints on mine?

Poetic Transcendence

Your riptide took me under
my last thoughts
such eyes beckoning
helplessly I drowned into you.

Yet you stayed with me
all those words we shared
surfacing into this world
we did this all before.

As the darkness finds me
your madness became mine
poetic transcendence
did you know it was me?

Turbulent Dénouement

Down the Road

Chills have helped me forget
breaking hearts still hold
chasing me down my road
like sand in the wind.

Everything is a poem now
dawn's shining moment
clouds racing with the rain
your eyes on mine.

How does time decide
who holds our keys
roads beckoning footprints
where will yours lead?

Lonely Shadows

Thoughts getting in my way
yesterday's tumbleweeds
they string me along
imprisoning yours.

Hopeful signposts eye me
surreptitiously becoming you
they wrap me inside out
laughing at our crazy.

Have you been here before
found your way home
escaped like a shadow
bookmarked our lonely?

Colliding Moments

Where we ever stood alone
thoughts our only company
they hug what was real
hoping to find us again.

Still roaming for your mirage
set against my cloudless sky
nightfall captures a glimpse
as moments collide inside us.

Eyes mirror what we think
shadows smile at us
won't you stay to tell me
what was on your mind?

Catching Fire

Catching your escaping look
even my own glimpsed
suddenly touching how
we knew our way home.

All alone without you
our songs mesmerize
catching fire inside us
only our heart remembers.

So many spaces painted
light shares who we are
you knew who I'd become
sleeping with your angel.

Ancient Shores

So we play an ancient song
as rain falls on footsteps
even when your tears
find mine upon today.

So we find what once was
as deserts cry
of days voices lyrical
singing within our hearts.

So we eveningtide what is
following our wildness
as shores slip away
till dawn remembers us.

Sad Poetry

Remember who you were
sunstruck rain on your eyes
laughter meant for us
eclipsing even the moon.

Sad poetry moves us
all alone till we find you
calling these moments
like they were always ours.

Will you find me tonight
across hidden lyrics
wake me up inside
become who I might be?

After Our Dance

Skies surreptitiously envelope you
coloring who I used to be
your magician laughs inside
as you nod and take my hand.

Glimpsing shadows try to run
but they're painted on us
like shared lipstick
kissing me goodbye.

Do you savor my dulcet
that look you blinked
fleeing afterthoughts
after our dance ends.

Baking Our Crazy

You look into my crazy
lips breath my name
even the sun fades away
shy under your shadow.

Searing touches ignite
a spell erotic wants us
coveting hands scramble
thoughts struggle free.

Lost amidst these wildfires
we strike deeper to be
as they take us away
I look into your crazy.

Leftover Lipstick

Startled you whisper my name
words follow cruising clouds
the day moments us for a look
sunrays tangle up your hair.

Desert beach sandcastles
searing mirages invite us
leftover lipstick smiles
remembering us.

In the candlelit shadows
your dance found mine
heavy bend glances
whispering your name.

Pandora's Embrace

Playfully we open Pandora's box
looking inside her
seeing us looking back
both of us sharing our deep.

Caught within her web
naked eyes taste us
we love how she feels
and another day beckons.

Flying through a moment
we've forgotten time
as she laughs with us
an angel settles down.

My Poem

Wrapping your words inside me
they dance in my silence
mesmerizing what's left
just saying how you feel.

When you're all alone
find mine strewn today
as you look for me
find me inside them.

When you've forgotten
how we'd laugh and cry
tell me what I was
when you were my poem.

Stringing Me Along

Writing these words
maybe you already knew
erasing what's forgotten
why do you string me along?

Stepping into our notes
like no one else knows
keeping our together
like we've been here before.

Wielding our beautiful
we stole one more kiss
waiting for our last
evaporating moment.

Twilight's Charm

Lonely farmhouse dirt roads
they hold my heart still
singing your sweet songs
till our sunlight fades.

Just as we find our way
as seasons beg to stay
so we meet ourselves again
cooking what we've made.

Twilight's gods charm our skies
remembering those eyes
lighting up eventide
as nightfall holds us still.

Sustaining Us

Your eyes piano mine
taking in everything
as we walk away
only your last note sustains.

Days fall in love with weeks
leaving me in silence
as your voice surfaces
only my mind sees you.

When you find me again
pictures line your walls
play me your favorite song
make us real once again.

Our Chill

Touch my skies with tomorrow
promise me you're real
and as the day takes us
forever my look into you.

Light glistening like smiles
laughter binding together
forgotten sighs hug us
rapt stolen breath escapes.

Bound like twin flames
we flower under the sun
even when we're gone
our chill touches us.

Silent Realizations

Beginnings' sweet moment
another universe opens up
you step into a new real
slipping on both together.

Dawning realization fills silence
as you learn who you are
kindness evokes memory
as you fly into novel skies.

New music captivates you
playing across your mind
a seamless blend becomes you
unifying your new universe.

Haunting Piano

Piano walks us through time
around our naïveté
haunting empathetic eyes
memorize our melody.

Her voice takes my hand
shows me your empty room
only photographs remain
lining walls inside my mind.

Sighs sweep past us now
into a storm we became
my hand remembers yours
a dance our fingers made up.

Coltrane's Ghost

Cymbals atmosphere the night
Coltrane's ghost lures us
in forgotten delicate time
another New York melody.

We sashay basking Harlem
a dance the night has earned
trumpeting lonely saxophones
as all eyes become yours.

Smoking blues evaporate
baking evening's chill
outside these naked streets
no one walks home alone.

Empty Shores

Light ebbs out from me
Surreal blankets starlit skies
Becoming my ghost
Lost sailors lure empty shores
When you once shared your waves here.

Becoming

Alone on the edge of the world
your touch
searing...

as the moment stretches
we lose ourselves
submerging...

under strange skies
a breath kept
laughing...

like we've always known
that first electric kiss
becoming...

when even a memory
seems more real than
how we lived it.

Mirroring You

Rain finds all of us now
underneath these stars
tears we've shared here
as you're already gone.

Far down apart from us
when you're ready for me
this rush feels so difficult
I only wanted you here.

I'm just a mirror seeing you
even as we're changing
breathing tides of sand
you were always safe inside.

Separate Shores

Strumming chords like they were us
evening atmosphere bakes
an ocean of sand waves breaks
frozen in different time.

I'd play you my song all night
whispering on separate shores
and as the tide takes us away
our sounds carry the night.

Your happy storms our beach
caught within a forgotten melody
and as we sing our lives in time
my own has awakened me.

Making Up Words

You knew it when we met
betting against fate
it's always like this
no one stays to say hello.

Friday fires bake delicious
crazy blue smiles kiss
when you want me
even cheap wine screams.

True light makes us laugh
slipping under our words
as they make us up
should we become them?

Sharing Moments

Time has a way of finding us
caught between atoms and stars
lonely thoughts keep us
as angels hold our hands.

Evanescing like morning dew
we disappear within the light
looking for who you are
another angel beside us.

We thread moments together
stitching our lives here
will you sit with me again
let me take your hand?

Imaginary Cowboys

Rain like you've never felt
along never ending roads
imaginary cowboys fade
you're on your own.

Consequences settle you
drifting through reason
piercing sunlight sears
you know what to do.

Realization tears myths
a momentary indiscretion
fables become you
we're never really alone.

Unused Words

Kindness like we know
time precious you share
when it's gone are we lost
like unused words in a poem?

If you close your eyes
make up what we'll will be
find your new voice
hold on to our dream.

Poetic apparitions haunt
soaring for light's thrill
even darkness descending
loves a human touch.

Meeting You

When you finally awaken
finding your voice
everyone stares back
embraced by a new sun.

Wielding a delicate flame
even your eyes flash fire
searing who you are here
no longer part of a dream.

Wonder wraps us together
a song no one's heard
like a first quickening
screaming you all your real.

Belief's Charm

Does light remember darkness
poised before awakening
even dreams cling to us
as we step into the sun

All we mirror is all we see
flowers climb around us
days of human touch
our only chance here

When you hold belief's charm
does change forget you
abandoning them
to become human?

Alone in Our Ocean of Night

Once we find ourselves
alone in our ocean of night
comforted by stars
terrified without your voice.

Cloaking lost hopes
we trust stealth to be
slipping between days
never fully awakened.

Tormented by lost reasons
memories try to smile
even as your songs sing
I wonder who you were.

Eyes of the Night

Melancholic waves shore us
uncharted glances remain
clouds touching our ocean
even our laughter tears.

We summer our snowstorm
freezing what we wanted
would you still stay
find that deserted beach.

Would we ever walk alone
just ahead of empty shadows
hands looking for a dance
lost in the eyes of the night.

Jealous Skies

Holding hands we knew
jealous skies stormed
laughter made us real
we knew who we'd become.

I would sing your song
walking inside our storm
no one noticed as we flew
sharing our wings.

Years have forgotten us
when rain imagined our tears
will you walk again
hold my hands to see me?

Unbroken Wings

Bound twin photons knew
finally becoming us
we soar in empty time
gathering new words to play.

Drinking in luminescence
we taste our desire
I wanna find your eyes
like you knew I would.

Love on unbroken wings
you carry our childlike moment
born in your light
who will she become?

Your Vibe

Dancing vibe binds us
Swept up in your beautiful
Caught within your light
We play our vibe all day long
Sharing ours as we come home

Fate

What is real today
Visions unveiling your fate
Memories we share
Caravanserai's night stand
Morning's laughs remembering.

Painting You

Welcome to our wild
We eat metaphors daily
Sipping life like wine
As we paint you in a poem
Making it up as we go.

Alone

Why does our light flee
when we look away
remembering such treasures
I got used to yours.

Embracing like minds
we saved ourselves each day
until I lost my way
alone without you.

You took my mind away
leaving only astonishment
as treasuring beautiful souls
I'm lost without yours.

We move from room to room
remembering our songs
inside your mind
they never let you go.

I know you keep them safe
every time we meet
your eyes would hug mine
because we're so alone.

We share fragile hearts
broken by searing madness
these memories kept
hold us both together.

Our Words

Your imagination steals mine
caught inside such gorgeous
even my piano fails me
as you dance in my light.

Wonder falls in step with me
she knows who we'll become
should I moment her real
will you stay in mine.

I've never shared my dark
so even as you hold me
delicate keys play us
reimagining my words.

Shores

Imagining we see vast spaces
covering who we'll become
alone yet unafraid of ourselves
stepping across to you.

Your look always flowers
touching songs no one knows
even as I read your eyes
loneliness has lost its shore.

Desert Skies

A song has stolen you
rapt skies your only home
days of crushing happy
anchors for yesterday.

Consequence rolls our dice
melodies bemuse us now
time keys what we love
today's lost doorways.

Oh if we knew the road
between galaxy's realms
would you sail with me
through this lonely desert?

Chasing Ladybugs

Who were we before
all alone on our own
untouched by your eyes
unknown by our light?

If I reach across to you
can you remember us
chasing pretty ladybugs
fearlessly diving into now?

All that we might become
would that you stay here
enthralled by my poem
as you write me yours?

Future Primitive

Alit within a desert storm
her eyes bent spacetime
flickering quantum consciousness
an oasis amidst our realms

In time to see the sun
we dance around life's tree
our song of the wind
circling astonishment

Future primitive beckons
soaring in your sky
leaving behind our magic
we embrace yours.

Dirty Work

Addicted to your times
crossroads stretch our legs
it's time to pay the keeper
I'm a fool to stay here.

Let the sun dress you
let our glitterati roam free
taste my goodbye look
I know what you want.

Darling we both love it
like a never ending rush
each time we play again
even dirty work is fun.

August's Gravity

Lover's shadows can't be
distilling moments
crazy eyes selfies
can you see mine?

August's gravity calls names
she remembers your smile
days when we'd dance
beckoning autumnal dust.

Your newborn wings stretch
touching farewells
time fell in love with us
even tomorrow says goodbye.

Close to the Edge

How thin our ice can be
when rain refuses to fall
when we risk it all
stay close to the edge.

Prayers of the wildness
a deepness inside us
love ricochets inside out
our inner keeper here.

Precious nonlinear time
our conscious thought
we were made for love
even when the ice breaks.

Your Dance

All alone in searing heat
you don't keep me dear
wildness has taken you
someone else beckons.

Rain has forsaken our sky
when I walk alone
we'd dance under them
a self-fulfilling prophecy.

Dangerous looks steal me
my night abandoned
I remember your look
no one else dances with me.

Hypnotic Tastes

Smoking like a sultry afterglow
our melt begs afterthoughts
crisscrossing fingers look for us
even as we're already gone.

Your look starving rapturous
like we've waited forever
mine steals another dance
slipping back to remind you.

Mesmerized we fall in step
our songs what we cannot say
hypnotic tastes fall all over us
relighting roads we never left.

Shadow Flames

Should you leave us
days without meaning
we both paint alone
your shadow falling on mine.

My songs written for you
they opened us both
love sings all alone
written within our flames.

Skies sear a troubled time
even as we piano us
lonely streetlights beckon
shadows only we can blanket.

Beside You

I've written about you
pages both of us lived
each moment we've laughed
time knows you wanted more

Take me back across yours
when we didn't know
our safe place
eyes told me everything.

Your beautiful scripted us
should we stay now
singing who we wanted
take us both home tonight.

Flamenco Fantasy

When you finally let go
freed to become your truth
will you recall our dark days
haunted alone as a stranger?

Apathy flees under your sun
fierce gazes hold us here
a touching couplet sings
how much you mean to me.

Brazillian flames torch passion
as time replays our skies
we flamenco fantasies
ghosting our hearts together.

Touching Real

Pretending we might be real
everyone else left
I found your memory
painted inside my eyes.

Mazes map my way back
pages of our songs
singing what we found
touching who we became.

Ripples beach our minds
tearing up lost thought
like days we couldn't stop
we were the only ones alive.

Made Up Words

Just your mind in mine
hands all over us
slipping inside our dreams
we walk beside them.

You stole my heartbeat
our laughter ringing true
clouds move to embrace us
even light reminds us.

Words we've made up
they litter our memories
poems only you've read
our hands all over them.

Torrent's Rapture

Slipping across to you
a weepingly delicious duet
a partner's dancing rapture
footsteps within our soul.

Emotion torrents whip us
eyes tied as one in step
musical ménage à trois
delight's soaring storm.

Our ballet allemande stirs
the hunt of our lives
of heartbeat rhythms
a dance only we bake.

Forever Song

Days pass like hours now
they steal us away
Mr Young's Cowgirls plays
washing over us like a wave.

California found me alone
she taught me your song
she loved to make me smile
time never mattered then.

We still play in the sand
as time rusts us away
all these words fall out
into our forever song.

Our Fate

We've known her mettle
Even storms find another
I've seen you before
Striking eyes that slay us all
Such is our fate to be yours.

Yesterday's Reign

Dust settles dénouements
our footprints confused
laughter runs just ahead
trying to catch up.

Stories seem like reruns
venturing into dreams
I write outside of time
so we can find us again.

We play our songs
threading our lives together
rereading us today
while yesterday reigns.

Taking Your Dénouement

We are all time travelers
skating in our moments
should we stop here
share our ice with yours?

Stepping across a pause
our gambits crisscross
laughing our concerns
we make us up again.

You read me delicious
unable to stop your bite
taking your dénouement
as I find yours mine.

Epilogue

Words

Words make us up
trying on our smile
they wonder if we're real
kissing our lips goodbye.

Freed from my mind
they rush into yours
rewriting past confusion
unlocking all your secrets.

They sing of a new song
embracing what we want
each pause a temptation
paragraphing our delicious.

Verde Mar is a pseudonym.